Godot 4
Game Development Projects

Second Edition

Build five cross-platform 2D and 3D games using
one of the most powerful open source game engines

Chris Bradfield

BIRMINGHAM—MUMBAI

Godot 4 Game Development Projects

Second Edition

Group Product Manager: Rohit Rajkumar
Publishing Product Manager: Kaustubh Manglurkar
Senior Content Development Editor: Feza Shaikh
Technical Editor: Simran Ali
Copy Editor: Safis Editing
Project Coordinator: Aishwarya Mohan
Proofreader: Safis Editing
Indexer: Hemangini Bari
Production Designer: Ponraj Dhandapani
Marketing Coordinators: Anamika Singh, Namita Velgekar, and Nivedita Pandey

First published: June 2018

Second edition: August 2023

Production reference: 1110723

Packt Publishing Ltd
Grosvenor House
11 St Paul's Square
Birmingham
B3 1RB UK.

ISBN 978-1-80461-040-4

www.packtpub.com

To Priya, for being a constant source of support and encouragement.

To my students at the Science Academy STEM Magnet for being my guinea pigs, and for teaching me how to be a better teacher.

-Chris Bradfield

Contributors

About the author

Chris Bradfield has worked in the internet technology space for more than 25 years. He has worked in the online gaming space for a number of successful MMOs and social gaming publishers in South Korea and the United States. Throughout his game industry career, he has served as a game designer, developer, product manager, and business development executive.

In 2012, he discovered a love for teaching and founded KidsCanCode to provide programming instruction and curricula to middle- and high-school students. He also produces video- and text-based tutorials and other learning resources for game development students around the world.

I would like to express my gratitude to Kenney Vleugels (@kenneyNL) for the 3D Minigolf tiles, skorpio for the spaceship art, Luis Zuno (@ansimuz), and for Sunny Land art for their work.

About the reviewer

In the land of Indonesia, **Isaiah Jamiel** stands as a masterful artisan skilled in the realms of .NET and Godot. Leading NTC Studios alongside Izra, Hansen, Sachio, Shannon, Della, and Yesika, he aspires to achieve success in the realm of game development. Jamiel's artistic talents extend beyond coding, as he breathes new life into traditional Indonesian music with his arrangements. Yet amidst his passion for code and music, his heart finds solace in the unwavering love he holds for his beloved Valerie and his cherished family. Isaiah Jamiel's unwavering commitment to blending innovation, artistry, and profound connections serves as the driving force behind his remarkable endeavors in both the realm of technology and the world of music.

Table of Contents

3

Space Rocks: Build a 2D Arcade Classic with Physics   49

4

Jungle Jump – Running and Jumping in a 2D Platformer   97

5

3D Minigolf: Dive into 3D by Building a Minigolf Course   143

6

Infinite Flyer 179

7

Next Steps and Additional Resources 207

Preface

This book is an introduction to the Godot game engine and its new version, 4. Godot 4 has a large number of new features and capabilities that make it a strong alternative to expensive commercial game engines. For beginners, it offers a friendly way to learn game development techniques. For more experienced developers, Godot is a powerful, customizable tool for bringing visions to life.

This book takes a project-based approach to learning how to use Godot. It consists of five projects, along with additional resources, that will help developers achieve a sound understanding of how to use Godot to build games.

Who this book is for

This book is for anyone who wants to learn how to make games using a modern game engine. New users and experienced developers alike will find it a helpful resource. Some programming experience is recommended.

What this book covers

This book is a project-based introduction to using the Godot game engine. Each of the five game projects builds on the concepts learned in the previous projects.

Chapter 1, Introduction to Godot 4.0 introduces the concept of game engines in general and Godot specifically, including how to download Godot and how to effectively use this book.

Chapter 2, Coin Dash – Build Your First 2D Game, is a small 2D game that demonstrates how to create scenes and work with Godot's node system. You'll learn how to navigate the Godot editor and write your first scripts in GDScript.

Chapter 3, Space Rocks: Build a 2D Arcade Classic with Physics, demonstrates working with physics bodies to create an *Asteroids*-style space game.

Chapter 4, Jungle Jump – Running and Jumping in a 2D Platformer, involves a side-scrolling platform game in the spirit of *Super Mario Bros.* You'll learn about kinematic bodies, animation states, and level design using tile maps.

Chapter 5, 3D Minigolf: Dive into 3D by Building a Minigolf Course, extends the previous concepts into three dimensions. You'll work with meshes, lighting, and camera control.

Chapter 6, Infinite Flyer, continues exploring 3D development, covering dynamic content, procedural generation, and more 3D techniques.

Chapter 7, Next Steps and Additional Resources, covers even more topics to explore once you've mastered the material in the five game projects. Look here for links and tips to further expand your game development skills.

To get the most out of this book

To best understand the example code in this book, you should have a general knowledge of programming, preferably with a modern, dynamically-typed language such as Python or JavaScript. If you're new to programming entirely, you may wish to review a beginner tutorial before diving into the game projects here.

Godot will run on any relatively modern PC running Windows, MacOS, or Linux operating systems.

If you are using the digital version of this book, we advise you to type the code yourself or access the code from the book's GitHub repository (a link is available in the next section). Doing so will help you avoid any potential errors related to the copying and pasting of code.

Download the example code files

You can download the example code files for this book from GitHub at `https://github.com/PacktPublishing/Godot-4-Game-Development-Projects-Second-Edition`. If there's an update to the code, it will be updated in the GitHub repository.

We also have other code bundles from our rich catalog of books and videos available at `https://github.com/PacktPublishing/`. Check them out!

Download the color images

We also provide a PDF file that has color images of the screenshots and diagrams used in this book. You can download it here: `https://packt.link/lY2hq`.

Conventions used

There are a number of text conventions used throughout this book.

`Code in text`: Indicates code words in text, database table names, folder names, filenames, file extensions, pathnames, dummy URLs, user input, and Twitter handles. Here is an example: "With Godot 4, you have an additional option: importing `.blend` files directly into your Godot project."

A block of code is set as follows:

```
shader_type canvas_item;

void fragment() {
    // Place fragment code here.
}
```

Bold: Indicates a new term, an important word, or words that you see onscreen. For instance, words in menus or dialog boxes appear in **bold**. Here is an example: "The first property is **Shader**, where you can choose **New Shader**. When you do, a **Create Shader** panel appears."

> **Tips or important notes**
> Appear like this.

Get in touch

Feedback from our readers is always welcome.

General feedback: If you have questions about any aspect of this book, email us at customercare@ packtpub.com and mention the book title in the subject of your message.

Errata: Although we have taken every care to ensure the accuracy of our content, mistakes do happen. If you have found a mistake in this book, we would be grateful if you would report this to us. Please visit www.packtpub.com/support/errata and fill in the form.

Piracy: If you come across any illegal copies of our works in any form on the internet, we would be grateful if you would provide us with the location address or website name. Please contact us at copyright@packt.com with a link to the material.

If you are interested in becoming an author: If there is a topic that you have expertise in and you are interested in either writing or contributing to a book, please visit authors.packtpub.com.

Share Your Thoughts

Once you've read, we'd love to hear your thoughts! Scan the QR code below to go straight to the Amazon review page for this book and share your feedback.

https://packt.link/r/1804610402

Your review is important to us and the tech community and will help us make sure we're delivering excellent quality content.

Download a free PDF copy of this book

Thanks for purchasing this book!

Do you like to read on the go but are unable to carry your print books everywhere?

Is your eBook purchase not compatible with the device of your choice?

Don't worry, now with every Packt book you get a DRM-free PDF version of that book at no cost.

Read anywhere, any place, on any device. Search, copy, and paste code from your favorite technical books directly into your application.

The perks don't stop there, you can get exclusive access to discounts, newsletters, and great free content in your inbox daily

Follow these simple steps to get the benefits:

1. Scan the QR code or visit the link below

https://packt.link/free-ebook/9781804610404

2. Submit your proof of purchase
3. That's it! We'll send your free PDF and other benefits to your email directly

1

Introduction to Godot 4.0

Whether it's a career goal or a recreational hobby, game development is a fun and rewarding endeavor. There's never been a better time to get started in game development. Modern programming languages and tools have made it easier than ever to build high-quality games and distribute them to the world. If you're reading this book, then you've set your feet on the path to making the game(s) of your dreams.

This book is an introduction to the Godot Game Engine and its new 4.0 version, which was released in 2023. Godot 4.0 has a large number of new features and capabilities that make it a strong alternative to expensive commercial game engines. For beginners, it offers a friendly way to learn game development fundamentals. For more experienced developers, Godot is a powerful, customizable, and *open* toolkit for bringing your visions to life.

This book takes a project-based approach that will introduce you to the fundamentals of the engine. It consists of five game projects that are designed to help you achieve a sound understanding of game development concepts and how they're applied in Godot. Along the way, you will learn how Godot works and absorb important techniques that you can apply to your own projects.

In this chapter, we'll cover the following topics:

- General advice for getting started
- What is a game engine?
- What is Godot?
- Downloading Godot
- Overview of the Godot UI
- Nodes and scenes
- Scripting in Godot

General advice

This section contains some general advice to readers, based on the author's experience as a teacher and lecturer. Keep these tips in mind as you work through the book, especially if you're very new to programming.

Try to follow the projects in the book in order. Later chapters may build on topics that were introduced in earlier chapters, where they are explained in more detail. When you encounter something that you don't remember, go back and review that topic in the earlier chapter. No one is timing you, and there's no prize for finishing the book quickly.

There is a lot of material to absorb here. Don't feel discouraged if you don't get it at first. The goal is not to become an expert in game development overnight – that's just not possible. Just like with any other skill – carpentry or a musical instrument, for example – it takes years of practice and study to develop proficiency. Repetition is the key to learning complex topics; the more you work with Godot's features, the more familiar and easier they will start to seem. Try repeating one of the earlier chapters after you reach the end. You'll be surprised at how much more you'll understand compared to the first time you read it.

If you're reading this as an e-book, resist the temptation to copy and paste the code. Typing the code yourself will engage your brain more actively. It's similar to how taking notes during a lecture helps you learn better than just listening, even if you never look back at the notes. If you're a slow typist, it will also help you work on your typing speed. In a nutshell: you're a programmer, so get used to typing code!

One of the biggest mistakes that new game developers make is taking on a bigger project than they can handle. It is very important to keep the scope of your project as small as possible when starting out. You will be much more successful (and learn more) if you finish two or three small games than if you have a large, incomplete project that has grown beyond your ability to manage.

You'll notice that the five games in the book follow this strategy very strictly. They are all small in scope, both for practical reasons – to fit reasonably into book-sized lessons – but also to remain focused on practicing the basics. As you build the game, you will likely find yourself thinking of additional features and gameplay elements right away. *What if the spaceship had upgrades? What if the character could do wall jumps?*

Ideas are great, but if you haven't finished the basic project yet, write them down and save them for later. Don't let yourself be sidetracked by one "cool idea" after another. Developers call this *feature creep*, meaning a list of features that never stops growing, and it's a trap that has led to many an unfinished project. Don't fall victim to it.

Finally, don't forget to take a break now and again. You shouldn't try and power through the whole book, or even one project, in just a few sittings. After each new concept, and especially after each chapter, give yourself time to absorb the new information before you dive into the next one. You'll find that you not only retain more information, but you'll probably enjoy the process more.

The secret to learning effectively

Here's the secret to getting the most out of these projects and increasing your skills in a way that makes them stick: at the end of each chapter, once you've finished building the game project, immediately delete it and start over. This time, try and re-create it without looking at the book. If you get stuck, just look at that part in the chapter, and then close the book again. If you really feel confident, try adding your own spin to the game – change some parts of the gameplay or add a new twist.

If you do this multiple times with each of the games, you'll be amazed at how less often you'll need to check the book. If you can make the projects in this book on your own without help, then you're surely ready to branch out and take on your original concepts.

Keep these tips in mind as you read through the following sections. In the next section, you'll learn what a game engine is and why game developers might want to choose to use one.

What is a game engine?

Game development is complex and involves a wide variety of knowledge and skills. To build a modern game, you need a great deal of underlying technology before you can make the actual game itself. Imagine that you had to build your computer and write your own operating system before you could even start programming. Game development would be a lot like that if you truly had to start from scratch and make everything that you need.

There are also a number of common needs that every game has. For example, no matter what the game is, it's going to need to draw things on the screen. If the code to do that has already been written, it makes more sense to reuse it than to create it all over again for every game. That's where game frameworks and engines come in.

A **game framework** is a set of libraries with helper code that assists in building the foundational parts of a game. It doesn't necessarily provide all the pieces, and you may still have to write a great deal of code to tie everything together. Because of this, building a game with a game framework can take more time than one built with a full game engine.

A **game engine** is a collection of tools and technologies designed to ease the process of game-making by removing the need to reinvent the wheel for each new game project. It provides a collection of commonly needed functionality that often would require a significant investment in time and effort to develop.

Here are some of the main features a typical game engine will provide:

- **Rendering (2D and 3D)**: Rendering is the process of displaying the game on the player's screen. A good rendering pipeline must take into account modern GPU support, high-resolution displays, and effects such as lighting, perspective, and viewports, all while maintaining a very high framerate.

- **Physics**: While a very common requirement, building a robust and accurate physics engine is a monumental task. Most games require some sort of collision detection and response system, and many need physics simulations, but few developers want to take on the task of writing one - especially if they have never tried to do so before!

- **Platform support**: In today's market, most developers want to be able to release their games on multiple platforms, such as desktops, consoles, mobile, and/or the web. A game engine provides a unified exporting process to publish games on multiple platforms without needing to rewrite game code or support multiple versions.

- **Common development environment**: By using the same unified interface to make multiple games, the developer doesn't have to re-learn a new workflow every time they start a new project.

In addition to these, there will be tools to assist with features such as networking, easing the process of managing images and sound, animations, debugging, and many more. Often, game engines will include the ability to import content from other tools, such as those used to create animations or 3D models.

Using a game engine allows the developer to focus on building their game rather than creating the underlying framework needed to make it work. For small or independent developers, this can mean the difference between releasing a game after one year of development instead of three, or even never at all.

There are dozens of popular game engines on the market today, such as Unity, Unreal Engine, and GameMaker Studio, just to name a few. An important fact to be aware of is that the majority of popular game engines are commercial products. They may or may not require any financial investment to get started, but they will require some kind of licensing and/or royalty payments if your game makes money. Whatever engine you choose, you need to carefully read the user agreement and make sure you understand what you are and are not allowed to do with the engine, and what hidden costs, if any, you may be responsible for.

On the other hand, some engines are non-commercial and *open source*, such as the Godot game engine, which is what this book is all about.

What is Godot?

Godot is a fully featured modern game engine, providing all of the features described in the previous section and more. It is also completely free and open source, released under the very permissive MIT license. This means there are no fees, no hidden costs, and no royalties to pay on your game's revenue. Everything you make with Godot 100% belongs to you, which is not the case with many commercial game engines that require an ongoing contractual relationship. For many developers, this is very appealing.

If you're not familiar with the concept of open source, community-driven development, this may seem strange to you. However, much like the Linux kernel, Firefox browser, and many other very well-known pieces of software, Godot is not developed by a company as a commercial product. Instead, a dedicated community of passionate developers donates their time and expertise to building the engine, testing and fixing bugs, producing documentation, and more.

As a game developer, the benefits of using Godot are many. Because it is unencumbered by commercial licensing, you have complete control over exactly how and where your game is distributed. Many commercial game engines restrict the types of projects you can make or require a much more expensive license to build games in certain categories, such as gambling.

Godot's open source nature also means there is a level of transparency that doesn't exist with commercial game engines. For example, if you find that a particular engine feature doesn't quite meet your needs, you are free to modify the engine itself and add the new features you need, with no permission required. This can also be very helpful when debugging a large project because you have full access to the engine's internal workings.

It also means that you can directly contribute to Godot's future. See *additional topics* in *Chapter 7* for more information about how you can get involved with Godot development.

Now that you have an understanding of what Godot is and how it can help you build a game, it's time to get started. In the next section, you'll see how to download Godot and set it up for use on your own computer.

Downloading Godot

You can download the latest version of Godot by visiting `https://godotengine.org/` and clicking **Download Latest**. This book is written for version 4.0. If the version you download has another number at the end (such as 4.0.3), that's fine – this just means that it includes updates to version 4.0 that fix bugs or other issues.

On the download page, you will also see a standard version and a .NET version. The .NET version is specially built to be used with the C# programming language. Don't download this one unless you plan to use C# with Godot. The projects in this book do not use C#.

Figure 1.1: The Godot download page

Unzip the downloaded file, and you'll have the Godot application. Optionally, you can drag it to your `Programs` or `Applications` folder, if you have one. Double-click the application to launch it and you'll see Godot's **Project Manager** window, which you'll learn about in the next section.

Alternate installation methods

There are a few other ways to get Godot on your computer besides downloading it from the Godot website. Note that there is no difference in functionality when installed this way. The following are merely alternatives for downloading the application:

- **Steam**: If you have an account on Steam, you can install Godot via the Steam desktop application. Search for Godot in the Steam store and follow the instructions to install it. You can launch Godot from the Steam application:

Figure 1.2: The Godot engine on Steam

- **Itch.io**: You can also download Godot from the popular `itch.io` website. Itch is a marketplace for independent game developers and creators. Search for Godot and download it from the provided links.

- **Package Managers**: If you're using one of the following operating system package managers, you can install Godot via its normal installation process. See the documentation for your package manager for details. Godot is available in these package managers:

  - Homebrew (macOS)

  - Scoop (Windows)

  - Snap (Linux)

Android and web versions

You will also see downloads available for Godot versions that run on Android and in your web browser. At the time of this writing, these versions are listed as "experimental" and may not be stable or fully functional. It is recommended that you use the desktop version of Godot, especially while you're learning.

Congratulations, you have successfully installed Godot on your computer. In the next section, you will see an overview of Godot's editor interface – the purposes of the various windows and buttons you'll use when working with the editor.

Overview of the Godot UI

Like most game engines, Godot has a unified development environment. This means that you use the same interface to work on all of the aspects of your game – code, visuals, audio, and so on. This section is an introduction to the interface and its parts. Take note of the terminology used here; it will be used throughout this book when referring to actions you'll take in the editor window.

Project Manager

The **Project Manager** window is the first window you'll see when you open Godot:

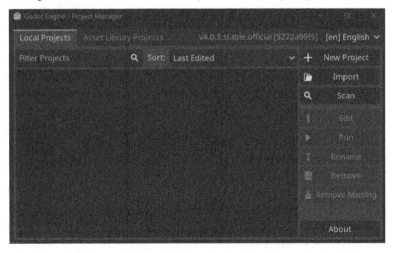

Figure 1.3: Project Manager

Opening Godot for the first time

The first time you open Godot, you won't have any projects yet. You'll see a pop-up window asking if you want to *explore official example projects in the Asset Library*. Select **Cancel**, and you'll see the **Project Manager** as it appears in the preceding screenshot.

In this window, you can see a list of your existing Godot projects. You can choose an existing project and click **Run** to play the game or **Edit** to work on it in the Godot editor. You can also create a new project by clicking **New Project**:

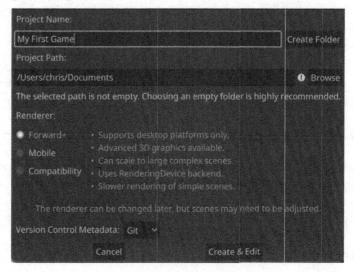

Figure 1.4: New project settings

Here, you can give the project a name and create a folder to store it in. Note the warning message – a Godot project is stored as a separate folder on the computer. All the files that the project uses must be located in this folder. This makes it convenient to share Godot projects because you only need to zip the project folder and you can be confident that another Godot user will be able to open it and not be missing any necessary data.

Renderer

When creating a new project, you also have the choice of **Renderer**. The three options represent the balance between advanced, high-performance graphics that require a modern desktop GPU, and compatibility with less-capable platforms such as mobile and older desktops. You can change this option later if you need, so it's OK to leave it as the default setting. If you later decide to build games for the mobile platform, the Godot documentation has a great deal of information regarding performance and rendering options. See *Chapter 7* for links and more information.

Choosing filenames

When you're naming your new project, there are a few simple rules you should try and follow that may save you some trouble in the future. Give your project a name that describes what it is – *Wizard Battle Arena* is a much better project name than *Game #2*. In the future, you'll never be able to remember which game number two was, so be as descriptive as possible.

You should also think about how you name your project folder and the files in it. Some operating systems are case-sensitive and distinguish between My_Game and my_game, while others do not. This can lead to problems if you move your project from one computer to another. For this reason, many programmers develop a standardized naming scheme for their projects, such as not using spaces in filenames and using _ between words. Regardless of what naming scheme you adopt, the most important thing is to be consistent.

Once you've created the project folder, the **Create Edit** button will open the new project in the editor window. Try it now: create a project called test_project.

Console window

If you're using a version of the Windows operating system, you'll also see a console window open when you run Godot. In this window, you can see warnings and errors produced by the engine and/or your project. This window doesn't appear on macOS or Linux, but you can see the console output if you launch the application from the command line using a Terminal program

---

Editor window

The following figure is a screenshot of the main Godot editor window. This is where you will spend most of your time when building projects in Godot. The editor interface is divided into several sections, each offering different functionality. The specific terminology for each section is described after *Figure 1.5*:

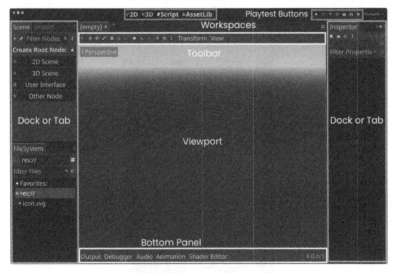

Figure 1.5: The Godot editor window

The main portion of the editor window is the *Viewport*. This is where you'll see the parts of your game as you're working on them.

In the top center of the window is a list of the *Workspaces* you can switch between when working on different parts of your game. You can switch between **2D** and **3D** mode, as well as **Script** mode, where you'll edit your game's code. **AssetLib** is a place where you can download add-ons and example projects contributed by the Godot community. See *Chapter 7* for more information about using the asset library.

Figure 1.6 shows the *toolbar* for the current workspace you're using. The icons here will change based on what kind of object you're working with:

Figure 1.6: Toolbar icons

The buttons in the upper-right *playtest* area are for launching the game and interacting with it when it's running:

Figure 1.7: Playtest buttons

On the left and right sides are the *Docks* or *Tabs* you can use to view and select game items and set their properties. On the bottom of the left-hand dock, you'll find the **FileSystem** tab. All the files in the project folder are shown here, and you can click on folders to open them and see what they contain. All resources in your project will be located relative to the `res://` path, which is the project's root folder. For example, a file path might look like this: `res://player/player.tscn`. This refers to a file in the `player` folder:

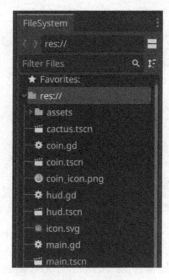

Figure 1.8: The FileSystem tab

At the top of the left-hand dock is the **Scene** tab, which shows the current scene you are working on in the viewport (more about scenes after *Figure 1.9*):

Figure 1.9: The Scene tab

On the right-hand side, you'll find a box labeled **Inspector**, where you can see and adjust the properties of your game objects.

As you work through the game projects in this book, you'll learn about the functionality of these items and become familiar with navigating the editor interface.

After reading this section, you should feel comfortable with the layout of the Godot editor window and the names of the elements you'll be seeing throughout the book. You're one step closer to finishing this introduction and getting started on a game. First, though, did you notice those items in *Figure 1.9*? Those are called nodes, and you'll find out what they're all about in the next section.

Learning about nodes and scenes

Nodes are the basic building blocks for creating games in Godot. A node is an object that can give you a variety of specialized game functions. A given type of node might display an image, play an animation, or represent a 3D model. The node contains a collection of properties, allowing you to customize its behavior. Which nodes you add to your project depends on what functionality you need. It's a modular system designed to give you flexibility in building your game objects.

The nodes you add are organized into a *tree* structure. In a tree, nodes are added as *children* of other nodes. A particular node can have any number of children, but only one *parent* node. When a group of nodes is collected into a tree, it is called a *scene*:

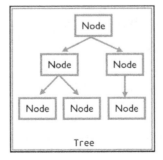

Figure 1.10: Nodes arranged in a tree

Scenes in Godot are typically used to create and organize the various game objects in your project. You might have a player scene that contains all the nodes and scripts that make the player's character work. Then, you might create another scene that defines the game's map: the obstacles and items that the player must navigate through. You can then combine these various scenes into the final game.

While nodes come with a variety of properties and functions, any node's behavior and capabilities can be extended by attaching a *script* to the node. This allows you to write code that makes the node do more than it can do in its default state. For example, you can add a `Sprite2D` node to display an image, but if you want that image to move or disappear when clicked, you'll need to add a script to create that behavior.

Nodes are powerful tools, and understanding them is the key to effectively building game objects in Godot. However, on their own, they can only do so much. It's still up to you to provide the game logic – the rules that objects in your game will follow. In the next section, you can see how that's done by writing code using Godot's scripting language.

Scripting in Godot

Godot provides two official languages for scripting nodes: **GDScript** and **C#**. GDScript is the dedicated built-in language, providing the tightest integration with the engine, and is the most straightforward to use. For those that are already familiar or proficient with C#, you can download a version that supports that language.

In addition to the two supported languages, Godot itself is written in C++, and you can get even more performance and control by extending the engine's functionality directly. See *Additional topics* in *Chapter 7* for information on using other languages and extending the engine.

All the games in this book will use GDScript. For the majority of projects, GDScript is the best choice of language. It is tightly integrated with Godot's **Application Programming Interface** (**API**) and is designed for rapid development.

About GDScript

GDScript's syntax is very closely modeled on the Python language. If you are familiar with Python already, you will find GDScript very familiar. If you are comfortable with another dynamic language, such as JavaScript, you should find it relatively easy to learn. Python is very often recommended as a good beginner language, and GDScript shares that user-friendliness.

This book assumes you have at least some programming experience already. If you've never coded before, you may find it a little more difficult. Learning a game engine is a large task on its own; learning to code at the same time means you've taken on a major challenge. If you find yourself struggling with the code in this book, you may find that working through an introductory programming lesson in a language such as Python or Javascript will help you grasp the basics.

Like Python, GDScript is a dynamically typed language, meaning you do not need to declare a variable's type when creating it, and it uses whitespace (indentation) to denote code blocks. Overall, the advantage of using GDScript for your game's logic is that, due to its tight integration with the engine, you write less code, which means faster development and fewer mistakes to fix.

To give you an idea of what GDScript looks like, here is a small script that causes a sprite to move from left to right across the screen at a given speed:

```
extends Sprite2D
var speed = 200

func _ready():
    position = Vector2(100, 100)

func_process(delta):
    position.x += speed * delta
```

If you've used other high-level languages such as Python before, this will look very familiar, but don't worry if this code doesn't make much sense to you yet. In the following chapters, you'll be writing lots of code, which will be accompanied by explanations of how it all works.

Summary

In this chapter, you were introduced to the concept of a game engine in general and to Godot in particular. Most importantly, you downloaded Godot and launched it!

You learned some important vocabulary that will be used throughout this book when referring to various parts of the Godot editor window. You also learned about the concepts of nodes and scenes, which are the fundamental building blocks of Godot.

You also received some advice on how to approach the projects in this book and game development in general. If you ever find yourself getting frustrated as you are working through this book, go back and reread the *General advice* section. There's a lot to learn, and it's OK if it doesn't all make sense the first time. You'll make five different games throughout this book, and each one will help you understand things a little bit more.

You're ready to move on to the next chapter, where you'll start building your first game in Godot.

Click **Project** -> **Project Settings** from the menu at the top. The settings window looks like this:

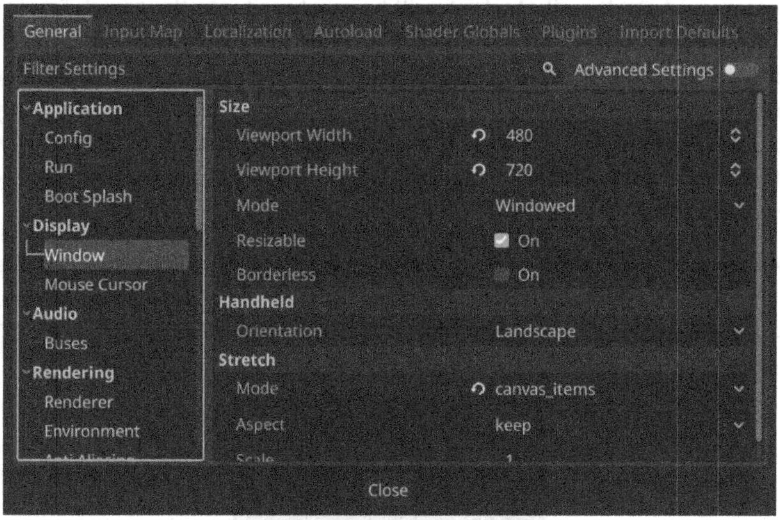

Figure 2.4: The Project Settings window

Look for the **Display** -> **Window** section and set **Viewport Width** to 480 and **Viewport Height** to 720, as shown in the preceding figure. Also in this section, under **Stretch**, set **Mode** to **canvas_items** and **Aspect** to **keep**. This will ensure that if a user resizes the game window, everything will scale appropriately and not become stretched or deformed. You can also uncheck the **Resizable** box under **Size** to prevent the window from being resized at all.

Congratulations! You've set up your new project, and you're ready to start making your first game. In this game, you'll make objects that move around in 2D space, so it's important to understand how objects are positioned and moved using 2D coordinates. In the next section, you'll learn how that works and how to apply it to your game.

Vectors and 2D coordinate systems

This section is a very brief overview of 2D coordinate systems and vector math as it's used in game development. Vector math is an essential tool in game development, so if you need a broader understanding of the topic, see Khan Academy's linear algebra series (`https://www.khanacademy.org/math/linear-algebra`).

When working in 2D, you'll use Cartesian coordinates to identify locations in the 2D plane. A particular position in 2D space is written as a pair of values, such as (4, 3), representing the position along the x and y axes, respectively. Any position in the 2D plane can be described in this way.

In 2D space, Godot follows the common computer graphics practice of orienting the *x* axis to the right and the *y* axis downward:

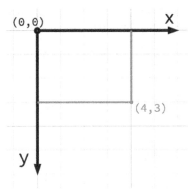

Figure 2.5: A 2D coordinate system

That's not what my math teacher taught me!

If you're new to computer graphics or game development, it might seem odd that the positive *y* axis points downward instead of upward, which you likely learned in math class. However, this orientation is very common in computer graphics applications.

Vectors

You can also think of the (4, 3) position as an *offset* from the (0, 0) point, or *origin*. Imagine an arrow pointing from the origin to the point:

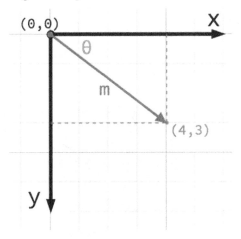

Figure 2.6: A 2D vector

This arrow is a *vector*. It represents a great deal of useful information, including the point's location, its distance or *length* (m), and its angle from the *x* axis (θ). More specifically, this type of vector is referred to as a *position* vector – that is, one that describes a position in space. Vectors can also represent movement, acceleration, or any other quantity that has a size and a direction.

In Godot, vectors have a wide array of uses, and you'll use them in every project in this book.

You should now have an understanding of how the 2D coordinate space works and how vectors can help to position and move objects. In the next section, you'll create the player object and use this knowledge to control its movement.

Part 1 – the player scene

The first scene you'll make is the player object. One of the benefits of creating a separate scene for the player (and other objects) is that you can test it independently, even before you've created other parts of a game. This separation of game objects will become more and more helpful as your projects grow in size and complexity. Keeping individual game objects separate from each other makes them easier to troubleshoot, modify, and even replace entirely without affecting other parts of the game. It also means your player can be reusable – you can drop this player scene into an entirely different game and it will work just the same.

Your player scene needs to do the following things:

- Display your character and its animations
- Respond to user input by moving the character
- Detect collisions with other game objects such as coins or obstacles

Creating the scene

Start by clicking the **Add/Create a New Node** button (the keyboard shortcut is *Ctrl + A*) and selecting an Area2D. Then, click on the node's name and change it to Player. Click **Scene -> Save Scene** (*Ctrl + S*) to save the scene.

Figure 2.7: Adding a node

Take a look at the **FileSystem** tab and note that the `player.tscn` file now appears. Whenever you save a scene in Godot, it will use the `.tscn` extension – this is the file format for Godot's scenes. The "t" in the name stands for "text" because these are text files. Feel free to take a look at it in an external text editor if you're curious, but you shouldn't edit one by hand; otherwise, you run the risk of accidentally corrupting the file.

You've now created the scene's **root** or top-level node. This node defines the overall functionality of the object. We've chosen `Area2D` because it's a 2D node, so it can move in 2D space, and it can detect overlap with other nodes, so we'll be able to detect the coins and other game objects. Choosing which node to use for a particular game object is your first important decision when designing your game objects.

Before adding any child nodes, it's a good idea to make sure you don't accidentally move or resize them by clicking on them. Select the `Player` node and hover your mouse on the icon next to the lock, **Group Selected Node(s)**:

Figure 2.8: Toggle the node grouping

The tooltip says **Make selected node's children not selectable.**, and that's good – it will help avoid mistakes. Click the button, and you'll see the same icon appear next to the player node's name:

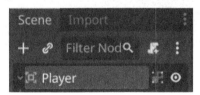

Figure 2.9: The node grouping icon

It's a good idea to always do this when creating a new scene. If an object's child nodes become offset or scaled, it can cause unexpected errors and be difficult to troubleshoot.

Sprite animation

With `Area2D`, you can detect when other objects overlap or run into a player, but `Area2D` doesn't have an appearance on its own. You'll also need a node that can display an image. Since the character has animations, select the player node and add an `AnimatedSprite2D` node. This node will handle the appearance and animations for the player. Note that there's a warning symbol next to the node.

Collision shape

When using `Area2D` or one of the other collision objects, you need to tell Godot what the shape of the object is. Its collision shape defines the region it occupies and is used to detect overlaps and/ or collisions. Shapes are defined by the various `Shape2D` types and include rectangles, circles, and polygons. In game development, this is sometimes referred to as a **hitbox**.

For convenience, when you need to add a shape to an area or physics body, you can add `CollisionShape2D` as a child. Then, you can select the type of shape you want and edit its size in the editor.

Add `CollisionShape2D` as a child of the `Player` node (make sure you don't add it as a child of `AnimatedSprite2D`). In the **Inspector** window, find the **Shape** property and click **<empty>** to select **New RectangleShape2D**.

Figure 2.16: Adding a collision shape

Drag the orange handles to adjust the shape's size to cover the sprite. Hint – if you hold the *Alt* key while dragging a handle, the shape will size symmetrically. You may have noticed that the collision shape is not centered on the sprite. That is because the sprite images themselves are not centered vertically. You can fix this by adding a small offset to `AnimatedSprite2D`. Select the node and look for the **Offset** property in the **Inspector** window. Set it to (0, -5).

Figure 2.17: Sizing the collision shape

When you're finished, your **Player** scene should look like this:

Figure 2.18: The Player node setup

Scripting the player

Now, you're ready to add some code to the player. Attaching a script to a node allows you to add additional functionality that isn't provided by the node itself. Select the `Player` node and click the **new script** button:

Figure 2.19: The new script button

In the **Attach Node Script** window, you can leave the default settings as they are. If you've remembered to save the scene, the script will be automatically named to match the scene's name. Click **Create**, and you'll be taken to the script window. Your script will contain some default comments and hints.

The first line of every script describes what type of node it is attached to. Just after that, you can start defining your variables:

```
extends Area2D

@export var speed = 350
var velocity = Vector2.ZERO
var screensize = Vector2(480, 720)
```

Using the `@export` annotation on the `speed` variable allows you to set its value in the **Inspector** window, just like any other node property. This can be very handy for values that you want to be able to adjust easily. Select the `Player` node, and you'll see the **Speed** property now appears in the

Inspector window. Any value you set in the **Inspector** window will override the 350 speed value you wrote in the script.

Figure 2.20: The exported variable in the Inspector window

As for the other variables, velocity will contain the character's movement speed and direction, while screensize will help set the limits of the character's movement. Later, you'll set this value automatically from the game's main scene, but for now, setting it manually will allow you to test that everything is working.

Moving the player

Next, you'll use the _process() function to define what the player will do. The _process() function is called on every frame, so you can use it to update elements of your game that you expect to change often. In each frame, you need the player to do three things:

- Check for keyboard input
- Move in the given direction
- Play the appropriate animation

First, you need to check the inputs. For this game, you have four directional inputs to check (the four arrow keys). Input actions are defined in **Project Settings** under the **Input Map** tab. In this tab, you can define custom events and assign keys, mouse actions, or other inputs to them. By default, Godot has events assigned to the keyboard arrows, so you can use them for this project.

You can detect whether an input action is pressed using Input.is_action_pressed(), which returns true if a key is held down and false if it is not. Combining the states of all four keys will give you the resulting direction of movement.

You can do this by checking all four keys separately using multiple if statements, but since this is such a common need, Godot provides a useful function called Input.get_vector() that will handle this for you – you just have to tell it which four inputs to use. Note the order that the input actions are listed in; get_vector() expects them in this order. The result of this function is a **direction vector** – a vector pointing in one of the eight possible directions resulting from the pressed inputs:

```
func _process(delta):
    velocity = Input.get_vector("ui_left", "ui_right",
        "ui_up", "ui_down")
    position += velocity * speed * delta
```

After that, you'll have a `velocity` vector indicating which direction to move in, so the next step will be to actually update the player's `position` using that velocity.

Click **Run Current Scene** (*F6*) at the top right, and check that you can move the player around using all four arrow keys.

You may notice that the player continues running off the side of the screen. You can use the `clamp()` function to limit the player's `position` to minimum and maximum values, preventing them from leaving the screen. Add these two lines next, immediately after the previous line:

```
    position.x = clamp(position.x, 0, screensize.x)
    position.y = clamp(position.y, 0, screensize.y)
```

About delta

The `_process()` function includes a parameter called `delta` that is then multiplied by `velocity`. What is `delta`?

The game engine attempts to run at a constant 60 frames per second. However, this can change due to computer slowdowns, either in Godot or from other programs running on your computer at the same time. If the frame rate is not consistent, then it will affect the movement of objects in your game. For example, consider an object that you want to move at 10 pixels every frame. If everything runs smoothly, this will mean the object moves 600 pixels in one second. However, if some of those frames take a bit longer, then there may have been only 50 frames in that second, so the object only moved 500 pixels.

Godot, like many game engines and frameworks, solves this by passing you a value called `delta`, which is the elapsed time since the previous frame. Most of the time, this will be very close to 0.016 seconds (around 16 milliseconds). If you then take your desired speed of 600 px/second and multiply it by `delta`, you'll get a movement of exactly 10 pixels. If, however, `delta` increased to 0.3 seconds, then the object would move 18 pixels. Overall, the movement speed remains consistent and independent of the frame rate.

As a side benefit, you can express your movement in units of pixels per second rather than pixels per frame, which is easier to visualize.

Choosing animations

Now that the player can move, you need to change which animation AnimatedSprite2D is playing, based on whether the player moves or stands still. The art for the run animation faces to the right, which means it needs to be flipped horizontally (using the **Flip H** property, which you can see in the **Inspector** window – go ahead and try toggling it) when moving to the left. Add this code to your _process() function after the movement code:

```
if velocity.length() > 0:
    $AnimatedSprite2D.animation = "run"
else:
    $AnimatedSprite2D.animation = "idle"
if velocity.x != 0:
    $AnimatedSprite2D.flip_h = velocity.x < 0
```

> **Getting nodes**
>
> When using the $ notation, the node name is *relative* to the node running the script. For example, $Node1/Node2 would refer to a node (Node2) that is a child of Node1, which is itself a child of the node that runs the script. Godot's autocomplete will suggest node names as you type. Note that if the name contains spaces, you must put quote marks around it – for example, $"My Node".

Note that this code takes a little shortcut. flip_h is a Boolean property, which means it can be true or false. A Boolean value is also the result of a comparison, such as <. Because of this, you can directly set the property equal to the result of the comparison.

Play the scene again and check that the animations are correct in each case.

Starting and ending the player's movement

The main scene will need to inform the player when the game has started and ended. To do that, add a start() function to the player, which will set the player's starting position and animation:

```
func start():
    set_process(true)
    position = screensize / 2
    $AnimatedSprite2D.animation = "idle"
```

Also, add a die() function to be called when the player hits an obstacle or runs out of time:

```
func die():
    $AnimatedSprite2D.animation = "hurt"
    set_process(false)
```

Using `set_process(false)` tells Godot to stop calling the `_process()` function every frame. Since the movement code is in that function, you'll no longer be able to move when the game is over.

Preparing for collisions

The player should detect when it hits a coin or an obstacle, but you haven't made those objects yet. That's OK because you can use Godot's *signal* functionality to make it work. Signals are a way for nodes to send out messages that other nodes can detect and react to. Many nodes have built-in signals to alert you when events occur, such as a body colliding or a button being pressed. You can also define custom signals for your own purposes.

Signals are used by *connecting* them to the node(s) that you want to listen for them. This connection can be made in the **Inspector** window or in code. Later in the project, you'll learn how to connect signals in both ways.

Add the following lines to the top of the script (after `extends Area2D`):

```
signal pickup
signal hurt
```

These lines declare custom signals that your player will **emit** when they touch a coin or obstacle. The touches will be detected by `Area2D` itself. Select the `Player` node, and click the **Node** tab next to the **Inspector** tab to see a list of signals the player can emit:

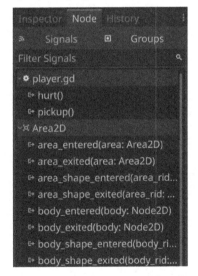

Figure 2.21: The node's list of signals

Note your custom signals there as well. Since the other objects will also be `Area2D` nodes, you'll want to use the `area_entered` signal. Select it and click **Connect**. In the window that pops up, click **Connect** again – you don't need to change any of those settings. Godot will automatically create a new function called `_on_area_entered()` in your script.

When connecting a signal, instead of having Godot create the function for you, you can also give the name of an existing function that you want to use instead. Toggle the **Make Function** switch off if you don't want Godot to create the function for you.

Add the following code to this new function:

```
func _on_area_entered(area):
    if area.is_in_group("coins"):
        area.pickup()
        pickup.emit()
    if area.is_in_group("obstacles"):
        hurt.emit()
        die()
```

Whenever another area object overlaps with the player, this function will be called, and that overlapping area will be passed in with the `area` parameter. The coin object will have a `pickup()` function that defines what the coin does when picked up (playing an animation or sound, for example). When you create the coins and obstacles, you'll assign them to the appropriate **group** so that they can be detected correctly.

To summarize, here is the complete player script so far:

```
extends Area2D

signal pickup
signal hurt

@export var speed = 350

var velocity = Vector2.ZERO
var screensize = Vector2(480, 720)


func _process(delta):
    # Get a vector representing the player's input
    # Then move and clamp the position inside the screen
    velocity = Input.get_vector("ui_left", "ui_right",
        "ui_up", "ui_down")
    position += velocity * speed * delta
    position.x = clamp(position.x, 0, screensize.x)
```

```
        position.y = clamp(position.y, 0, screensize.y)

        # Choose which animation to play
        if velocity.length() > 0:
            $AnimatedSprite2D.animation = "run"
        else:
            $AnimatedSprite2D.animation = "idle"

        if velocity.x != 0:
            $AnimatedSprite2D.flip_h = velocity.x < 0

    func start():
        # This function resets the player for a new game
        set_process(true)
        position = screensize / 2
        $AnimatedSprite2D.animation = "idle"

    func die():
        # We call this function when the player dies
        $AnimatedSprite2D.animation = "hurt"
        set_process(false)

    func _on_area_entered(area):
        # When we hit an object, decide what to do
        if area.is_in_group("coins"):
            area.pickup()
            pickup.emit()
        if area.is_in_group("obstacles"):
            hurt.emit()
            die()
```

You've completed setting up the player object, and you've tested that the movement and animations work correctly. Before you move on to the next step, review the player scene setup and the script, and make sure you understand what you've done and why. In the next section, you'll make some objects for the player to collect.

Part 2 – the coin scene

In this part, you'll make coins for the player to collect. This will be a separate scene, describing all the properties and behavior of a single coin. Once saved, the main scene will load this one and create multiple **instances** (that is, copies) of it.

Select **HCenter Wide** from the layout menu:

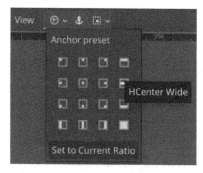

Figure 2.26: Positioning the message

The label now spans the width of the screen and is centered vertically. The **Text** property sets what text the label displays. Set it to **Coin Dash!**, and set **Horizontal Alignment** and **Vertical Alignment** both to **Center**.

The default font for Label nodes is very small and unattractive, so the next step is to assign a custom font. In the **Label Settings** property, select **New LabelSettings** and then click it to expand.

From the **FileSystem** tab, drag the Kenney Bold.ttf font file and drop it into the **Font** property, and then set **Size** to **48**. You can also improve the appearance by adding a shadow – try the settings shown in the following screenshot, or experiment with your own:

Figure 2.27: Font settings

Score and time display

The top of the HUD will display the player's score and the time remaining on the clock. Both of these will be Label nodes, arranged at opposite sides of the game screen. Rather than position them separately, you'll use a **container** node to manage their positions.

Containers

Godot's Container nodes automatically arrange the positions and sizes of their child Control nodes (including other containers). You can use them to add padding around elements, keep them centered, or arrange them in rows and columns. Each type of Container has special properties that control how they arrange their children.

Remember that containers automatically arrange their children. If you try to move or resize a Control that's inside a Container node, you'll get a warning from the editor. You can manually arrange controls *or* arrange them with a container, but not both.

Score and time display

To manage the score and time labels, add a MarginContainer node to the HUD. Use the layout menu to set the anchors to **Top Wide**. In the **Theme Overrides/Constants** section of the **Inspector** window, set the four **Margin** properties to 10. This will add some padding so that the text isn't against the edge of the screen.

Since the score and time labels will use the same font settings as Message, you can save time by duplicating it. Select Message and press *Ctrl + D* twice to create two duplicate labels. Drag them both and drop them onto MarginContainer to make them its children. Name one child Score and the other Time, and set the **Text** property to **0** for both. Set **Vertical Alignment** to **Center** on both, and **Horizontal Alignment** to **Right** on Score but **Left** on Time.

Updating the UI via GDScript

Add a script to the HUD node. This script will update the UI elements when their properties need to change, such as updating the Score text whenever a coin is collected. See the following code:

```
extends CanvasLayer

signal start_game

func update_score(value):
    $MarginContainer/Score.text = str(value)

func update_timer(value):
    $MarginContainer/Time.text = str(value)
```

The Main scene's script will call these two functions to update the display whenever there is a change in a value. For the Message label, you also need a timer to make it disappear after a brief period.

Add a `Timer` node as a child of HUD, and set **Wait Time** to 2 seconds and **One Shot** to **On**. This ensures that, when started, the timer will only run once, rather than repeating. Add the following code:

```
func show_message(text):
    $Message.text = text
    $Message.show()
    $Timer.start()
```

In this function, you will display the message and start the timer. To hide the message, connect the `timeout` signal of `Timer` (remember that it will automatically create the new function):

```
func _on_timer_timeout():
    $Message.hide()
```

Using buttons

Add a `Button` node to HUD and change its name to `StartButton`. This button will be displayed before the game starts, and when clicked, it will hide itself and send a signal to the `Main` scene to start the game. Set the **Text** property to **Start**, then scroll down to **Theme Overrides/Fonts**, and set the font as you did with `Message`.

In the layout menu, choose **Center Bottom** to center the button at the bottom of the screen.

When a button is pressed, it emits a signal. In the **Node** tab for `StartButton`, connect the `pressed` signal:

```
func _on_start_button_pressed():
    $StartButton.hide()
    $Message.hide()
    start_game.emit()
```

Game over

The final task for your UI script is to react to the game ending:

```
func show_game_over():
    show_message("Game Over")
    await $Timer.timeout
    $StartButton.show()
    $Message.text = "Coin Dash!"
    $Message.show()
```

In this function, you need the **Game Over** message to be displayed for two seconds and then disappear, which is what `show_message("Game Over")` does. However, you then want to show the start button and game title once the message has disappeared. The `await` command pauses the execution of a function until the given node (`Timer`) emits a given signal (`timeout`). Once the signal is received, the function continues, and everything will be returned to its initial state so that you can play again.

Adding HUD to Main

The next task is to set up the communication between Main and HUD. Add an instance of HUD to Main. In Main, connect the timeout signal of GameTimer and add the following so that every time GameTimer times out (every second), the remaining time is reduced:

```
func _on_game_timer_timeout():
    time_left -= 1
    $HUD.update_timer(time_left)
    if time_left <= 0:
        game_over()
```

Next, select the instance of Player in Main and connect its pickup and hurt signals:

```
func _on_player_hurt():
    game_over()


func _on_player_pickup():
    score += 1
    $HUD.update_score(score)
```

Several things need to happen when the game ends, so add the following function:

```
func game_over():
    playing = false
    $GameTimer.stop()
    get_tree().call_group("coins", "queue_free")
    $HUD.show_game_over()
    $Player.die()
```

This function halts the game and also uses call_group() to remove all remaining coins by calling queue_free() on each of them.

Finally, pressing StartButton needs to activate Main's new_game() function. Select the instance of HUD and connect its start_game signal:

```
func _on_hud_start_game():
    new_game()
```

Make sure you've removed new_game() from Main's _ready() function (remember, that was only there to test), and add these two lines to new_game():

```
$HUD.update_score(score)
$HUD.update_timer(time_left)
```

Now, you can play the game! Confirm that all parts are working as intended – the score, the countdown, the game ending and restarting, and so on. If you find a part that's not working, go back and check the step where you created it, as well as the step(s) where it may have been connected to the rest of the game. A common mistake is to forget to connect one of the many signals you used in different parts of the game.

Once you've played the game and confirmed that everything works correctly, you can move on to the next section, where you can add a few additional features to round out the game experience.

Part 5 – finishing up

Congratulations on creating a complete, working game! In this section, you'll add a few extra things to the game to make it a little more exciting. Game developers use the term **juice** to describe the things that make a game feel good to play. Juice can include things such as sound, visual effects, or any other addition that adds to the player's enjoyment, without necessarily changing the nature of the gameplay.

Visual effects

When you pick up the coins, they just disappear, which is not very appealing. Adding a visual effect will make it much more satisfying to collect lots of coins.

What is a tween?

A **tween** is a way to **interpolate** (change gradually) some value over time using a particular mathematical function. For example, you might choose a function that steadily changes a value or one that starts slow but ramps up in speed. Tweening is also sometimes referred to as **easing**. You can see animated examples of lots of tweening functions at https://easings.net/.

When using a tween in Godot, you can assign it to alter one or more properties of a node. In this case, you're going to increase the scale of the coin and also cause it to fade out using the **Modulate** property. Once the tween has finished its job, the coin will be deleted.

However, there's a problem. If we don't remove the coin immediately, then it's possible for the player to move onto the coin again – triggering the area_entered signal a second time and registering it as a second pickup. To prevent this, you can disable the collision shape so that the coin can't trigger any further collisions.

Your new pickup() function should look like this:

```
func pickup():
    $CollisionShape2d.set_deferred("disabled", true)
    var tw = create_tween().set_parallel().
        set_trans(Tween.TRANS_QUAD)
    tw.tween_property(self, "scale", scale * 3, 0.3)
    tw.tween_property(self, "modulate:a", 0.0, 0.3)
```

```
        await tw.finished
        queue_free()
```

That's a lot of new code, so let's break it down:

First, `CollisionShape2D`'s `disabled` property needs to be set to `true`. However, if you try setting it directly, Godot will complain. You're not allowed to change physics properties while collisions are being processed; you have to wait until the end of the current frame. That's what `set_deferred()` does.

Next, `create_tween()` creates a tween object, `set_parallel()` says that any following tweens should happen at the same time, instead of one after another, and `set_trans()` sets the transition function to the "quadratic" curve.

After that come two lines that set up the tweening of the properties. `tween_property()` takes four parameters – the object to affect (`self`), the property to change, the ending value, and the duration (in seconds).

Now, when you run the game, you should see the coins playing the effect when they're picked up.

Sound

Sound is an important but often neglected piece of game design. Good sound design can add a huge amount of juice to your game for a very small amount of effort. Sounds can give a player feedback, connect them emotionally to the characters, or even be a direct part of gameplay ("you hear footsteps behind you").

For this game, you're going to add three sound effects. In the `Main` scene, add three `AudioStreamPlayer` nodes and name them `CoinSound`, `LevelSound`, and `EndSound`. Drag each sound from the `res://assets/audio/` folder into the corresponding node's **Stream** property.

To play a sound, you call the `play()` function on the node. Add each of the following lines to play the sounds at the appropriate times:

- `$CoinSound.play()` to `_on_player_pickup()`
- `$EndSound.play()` to `game_over()`
- `$LevelSound.play()` to `spawn_coins()` (but not inside the loop!)

Powerups

There are many possibilities for objects that give the player a small advantage or powerup. In this section, you'll add a powerup item that gives the player a small time bonus when collected. It will appear occasionally for a short time, and then disappear.

Add a `Timer` node to the `Coin` scene and then add this to the coin's script:

```
func _ready():
    $Timer.start(randf_range(3, 8))
```

Then, connect the `Timer`'s `timeout` signal and add this:

```
func _on_timer_timeout():
    $AnimatedSprite2d.frame = 0
    $AnimatedSprite2d.play()
```

Try running the game and watching the coins animate. It's a nice visual effect for a very small amount of effort, at least on the part of the programmer –the artist had to draw all those frames! You'll notice a lot of effects like this in professional games. Although subtle, the visual appeal makes for a much more pleasing experience.

Obstacles

Finally, the game can be made more challenging by introducing an obstacle that the player must avoid. Touching the obstacle will end the game.

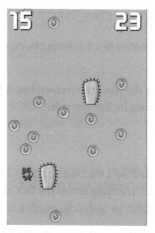

Figure 2.29: Example game with obstacles

Create a new `Area2D` scene and name it `Cactus`. Give it `Sprite2D` and `CollisionShape2D` children. Drag the cactus texture from **FileSystem** into the **Texture** property of `Sprite2D`. Add `RectangleShape2D` to the collision shape and size it so that it covers the image. Remember when you added `if area.is_in_group("obstacles"?)` to the player code? Add `Cactus` to the `obstacles` group using the **Node** tab. Play the game and see what happens when you run into the cactus.

You may have spotted a problem – coins can spawn on top of the cactus, making them impossible to pick up. When the coin is placed, it needs to move if it detects that it's overlapping with the obstacle. In the `Coin` scene, connect its `area_entered` signal and add the following:

```
func _on_area_entered(area):
    if area.is_in_group("obstacles"):
        position = Vector2(randi_range(0, screensize.x),
            randi_range(0, screensize.y))
```

If you added the `Powerup` object from the previous section, you'll need to do the same in its script.

Play the game, and test that the objects all spawn correctly and that they don't overlap with an obstacle. Running into an obstacle should end the game.

Do you find the game challenging or easy? Before moving on to the next chapter, take some time to think about other things you might add to this game. Go ahead and see whether you can add them, using what you've learned so far. If not, write them down and come back later, after you've learned some more techniques in the following chapters.

Summary

In this chapter, you learned the basics of the Godot Engine by creating a small 2D game. You set up a project and created multiple scenes, worked with sprites and animations, captured user input, used **signals** to communicate between nodes, and created a UI. The things you learned in this chapter are important skills that you'll use in any Godot project.

Before moving to the next chapter, look through the project. Do you know what each node does? Are there any bits of code that you don't understand? If so, go back and review that section of the chapter.

Also, feel free to experiment with the game and change things around. One of the best ways to get a good feel for what different parts of the game do is to change them and see what happens.

Remember the tip from *Chapter 1*? If you really want to advance your skills quickly, close this book, start a new Godot project, and try to make *Coin Dash* again without peeking. If you have to look in the book, it's OK, but try to only look for things once you've tried to figure out how to do it yourself.

In the next chapter, you'll explore more of Godot's features and learn how to use more node types by building a more complex game.

3

Space Rocks: Build a 2D Arcade Classic with Physics

By now, you should be getting more comfortable with working in Godot: adding nodes, creating scripts, modifying properties in the Inspector, and so on. If you find yourself stuck or feeling like you don't remember how something is done, you can jump back to a project where it was first explained. As you repeat the more common actions in Godot, they'll start to feel more and more familiar. At the same time, each chapter will introduce you to more nodes and techniques to expand your understanding of Godot's features.

In this project, you'll make a space shooter game similar to the arcade classic *Asteroids*. The player will control a ship that can rotate and move in any direction. The goal will be to avoid the floating "space rocks" and shoot them with the ship's laser. Here's a screenshot of the final game:

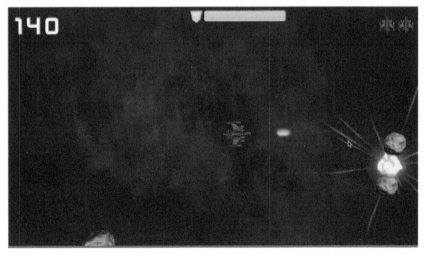

Figure 3.1: Space Rocks screenshot

You'll learn about the following key topics in this project:

- Using custom input actions
- Physics using `RigidBody2D`
- Organizing game logic with finite state machines
- Building a dynamic, scalable UI
- Sound and music
- Particle effects

Technical requirements

Download the game assets from the following link below and unzip them into your new project folder: `https://github.com/PacktPublishing/Godot-4-Game-Development-Projects-Second-Edition/tree/main/Downloads`

You can also find the complete code for this chapter on GitHub at: `https://github.com/PacktPublishing/Godot-4-Game-Development-Projects-Second-Edition/tree/main/Chapter03%20-%20Space%20Rocks`

Setting up the project

Create a new project and download the project assets from the following URL: `https://github.com/PacktPublishing/Godot-4-Game-Development-Projects-Second-Edition/tree/main/Downloads`.

For this project, you'll set up custom input actions in the **Input Map**. Using this feature, you can define custom input events and assign different keys, mouse events, or other inputs to them. This allows more flexibility in designing your game, as your code can be written to respond to the "jump" input, for example, without needing to know exactly what key and/or button the user pressed to make that event happen. This allows you to make the same code work on different devices, even if they have different hardware. In addition, since many gamers expect to be able to customize a game's inputs, this enables you to provide that option to the user as well.

To set up the inputs for this game, open **Project | Project Settings** and select the **Input Map** tab.

You'll need to create four new input actions: `rotate_left`, `rotate_right`, `thrust`, and `shoot`. Type the name of each action into the **Add New Action** box and hit *Enter* or click the **Add** button. Make sure you type the names exactly as shown since they'll be used in code later.

Then, for each action, click the + button to its right. In the pop-up window, you can manually select a specific type of input, or you can press the physical button and Godot will detect it. You can add multiple inputs to each action. For example, to allow players to use both the arrow keys and the WASD keys, the setup will look like this:

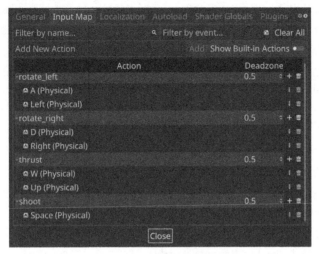

Figure 3.2: Input actions

If you have a gamepad or other controller connected to your computer, you can also add its inputs to the actions in the same way.

> **Note**
>
> We're only considering button-style inputs at this stage, so while you'll be able to use a D-pad for this project, using an analog joystick would require changes to the project's code.

Rigid body physics

In game development, you often need to know when two objects in the game space intersect or come into contact. This is known as **collision detection**. When a collision is detected, you typically want something to happen. This is known as **collision response**.

Godot offers three kinds of physics bodies, grouped under the `PhysicsBody2D` node type:

- `StaticBody2D`: A static body is one that is not moved by the physics engine. It participates in collision detection but does not move in response. This type of body is most often used for objects that are part of the environment or do not need to have any dynamic behavior, such as walls or the ground.

- `RigidBody2D`: This is the physics body that provides simulated physics. This means that you don't control a `RigidBody2D` physics body's position directly. Instead, you apply forces to it (gravity, impulses, and so on) and Godot's built-in physics engine calculates the resultant movement, including collisions, bouncing, rotating, and other effects.

- CharacterBody2D: This body type provides collision detection but no physics. All movement must be implemented in code, and you must implement any collision response yourself. Kinematic bodies are most often used for player characters or other actors that require *arcade-style* physics rather than realistic simulation, or when you need more precise control over how the body moves.

Understanding when to use a particular physics body type is a big part of building your game. Using the right type can simplify your development, while trying to force the wrong node to do the job can lead to frustration and poor results. As you work with each type of body, you'll come to learn their pros and cons and get a feel for when they can help build what you need.

In this project, you'll be using the RigidBody2D node for the ship as well as the rocks themselves. You'll learn about the other body types in later chapters.

Individual RigidBody2D nodes have many properties you can use to customize their behavior, such as **Mass**, **Friction**, or **Bounce**. These properties can be set in the Inspector.

Rigid bodies are also affected by global properties, which can be set in **Project Settings** under **Physics | 2D**. These settings apply to all bodies in the world.

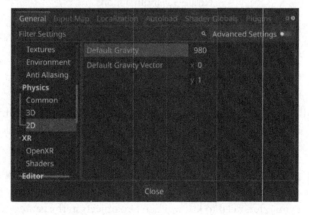

Figure 3.3: Project physics settings

In most cases, you won't need to modify these settings. However, note that by default, gravity has a value of 980 and a direction of (0, 1), or downward. If you want to change the world's gravity, you can do that here.

If you click the **Advanced Settings** toggle in the upper right of the **Project Settings** window, you'll see many advanced configuration values for the physics engine. You should be aware of two of them in particular: **Default Linear Damp** and **Default Angular Damp**. These properties control how quickly a body will lose forward speed and rotation speed, respectively. Setting them to lower values will make the world feel frictionless, while using larger values will make it feel like your objects are moving through mud. This can be a great way to apply different movement styles to suit various game objects and environments.

> **Area physics override**
>
> `Area2D` nodes can also be used to influence rigid body physics by using their **Space Override** property. Custom gravity and damping values will then be applied to any bodies that enter the area.

Since this game will be taking place in outer space, gravity won't be needed, so set **Default Gravity** to 0. You can leave the other settings as they are.

That completes the project setup tasks. It's a good idea to look back through this section and make sure you didn't miss anything, since the changes you've made here will affect the behavior of many game objects. You'll see this in the next section, where you'll make the player's ship.

The player's ship

The player's ship is the heart of this game. Most of the code you'll write for this project will be about making the ship work. It will be controlled in the classic "Asteroids style, with left/right rotation and forward thrust. The player will also be able to fire the laser and destroy floating rocks.

Figure 3.4: The player's ship

Body and physics setup

Create a new scene and add a `RigidBody2D` named `Player` as the root node, with `Sprite2D` and `CollisionShape2D` children. Add the `res://assets/player_ship.png` image to the **Texture** property of the `Sprite2D`. The ship image is quite large, so set the **Scale** property of the `Sprite2D` to (0.5, 0.5) and **Rotation** to 90.

Figure 3.5: Player sprite settings

Sprite orientation

The image for the ship is drawn pointing upward. In Godot, a rotation of 0 degrees points to the right (along the x-axis). This means that you need to rotate the sprite so that it will match the body's direction. If you use art that is drawn in the correct orientation, you can avoid this step. However, it's very common to find art that's drawn in an upward orientation, so you should know what to do.

In the **Shape** property of the `CollisionShape2D`, add a `CircleShape2D` and scale it to cover the image as closely as possible.

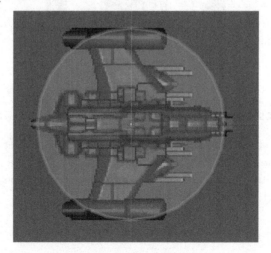

Figure 3.6: Player collision shape

The player ship is drawn in a pixel art style, but if you zoom in, you may notice it looks vary blurred and "smoothed out." Godot's default filter setting for drawing textures uses this smoothing technique, which looks good with some art, but typically isn't wanted for pixel art. You can set the filtering individually on each sprite (in the **CanvasItem** section), or you can set it globally in **Project Settings**.

Open **Project Settings** and check the **Advanced Settings** toggle, and then find the **rendering/textures** section. Near the bottom, you'll see two settings for **Canvas Textures**. Set **Default Texture Filter** to **Nearest**.

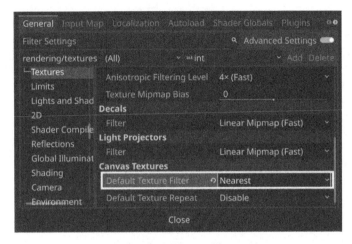

Figure 3.7: Default Texture Filter settings

Save the scene. When working on larger-scale projects, it is recommended to organize your scenes and scripts into folders based on each game object rather than saving them all in the root project folder. For example, if you make a "player" folder, you can save all player-related files there. This makes it easier to find and modify your various game objects. While this project is relatively small – you'll only have a few scenes – it's a good habit to adopt as your projects grow in size and complexity.

State machines

The player's ship can be in a number of different states during gameplay. For example, when *alive*, the ship is visible and can be controlled by the player, but it is vulnerable to being hit by rocks. On the other hand, when *invulnerable*, the ship should appear semi-transparent, and it is immune to damage.

One way that programmers often handle situations like this is to add Boolean variables, or *flags*, to the code. For example, the `invulnerable` flag is set to `true` when the player first spawns, or `alive` is set to `false` when the player is dead. However, this can lead to errors and strange situations when, for some reason, both `alive` and `invulnerable` are set to `false` at the same time. What happens when a rock hits the player in this situation? It would be better if the ship could only be in one clearly defined state at a time.

A solution to this problem is to use a **finite state machine** (**FSM**). When using an FSM, an entity can only be in one state at a given time. To design your FSM, you define a number of states and what events or actions can cause a transition from one state to another.

The following diagram depicts the FSM for the player's ship:

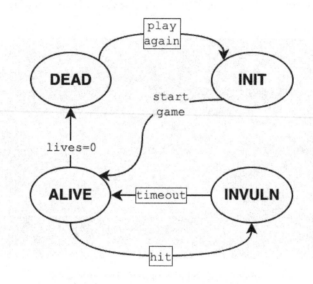

Figure 3.8: State machine diagram

There are four states, shown by the ovals, and the arrows indicate what transitions can occur between states, as well as what triggers the transition. By checking the current state, you can decide what the player is allowed to do. For example, in the **DEAD** state, don't allow input, or in the **INVULNERABLE** state, allow movement but don't allow shooting.

Advanced FSM implementations can become quite complex, and the details are beyond the scope of this book (see the *Appendix* for further reading). In the purest sense, you won't be creating a true FSM here, but for the purposes of this project, it will be sufficient to illustrate the concept and keep you from running into the Boolean flag problem.

Add a script to the `Player` node and start by creating the skeleton of the FSM implementation:

```
extends RigidBody2D

enum {INIT, ALIVE, INVULNERABLE, DEAD}
var state = INIT
```

An **enum** (short for "enumeration") is a convenient way to create a set of constants. The enum statement in the preceding code is equivalent to writing the following code:

```
const INIT = 0
const ALIVE = 1
const INVULNERABLE = 2
const DEAD = 3
```

Next, create the change_state() function to handle state transitions:

```
func _ready():
    change_state(ALIVE)

func change_state(new_state):
    match new_state:
        INIT:
            $CollisionShape2D.set_deferred("disabled",
                true)
        ALIVE:
            $CollisionShape2D.set_deferred("disabled",
                false)
        INVULNERABLE:
            $CollisionShape2D.set_deferred("disabled",
                true)
        DEAD:
            $CollisionShape2D.set_deferred("disabled",
                true)
    state = new_state
```

Whenever you need to change the state of the player, you'll call the change_state() function and pass it the value of the new state. Then, by using a match statement, you can execute whatever code should accompany the transition to the new state or disallow it if you don't want that transition to happen. To illustrate this, the CollisionShape2D node is being enabled/disabled by the new state. In _ready(), we set ALIVE as the initial state – this is for testing, but we'll change it to INIT later.

Adding player controls

Add the following variables at the top of the script:

```
@export var engine_power = 500
@export var spin_power = 8000

var thrust = Vector2.ZERO
var rotation_dir = 0
```

engine_power and spin_power control how fast the ship can accelerate and turn. thrust represents the force being applied by the engine: either (0, 0) when coasting or a vector pointing forward when the engine is on. rotation_dir represents in which direction the ship is turning so that you can apply a *torque* or rotational force.

As we saw earlier in **Project Settings**, the physics engine provides some *damping*, which reduces a body's velocity and spin. In space, there's no friction, so for realism, there shouldn't be any damping at all. However, for the classic arcade feel, it's preferable that the ship should stop when you let go of the keys. In the Inspector, set **Linear/Damp** to 1 and **Angular/Damp** to 5. You can adjust these later to change how the ship handles.

The next step is to detect the input and move the ship:

```
func _process(delta):
    get_input()

func get_input():
    thrust = Vector2.ZERO
    if state in [DEAD, INIT]:
        return
    if Input.is_action_pressed("thrust"):
        thrust = transform.x * engine_power
    rotation_dir = Input.get_axis("rotate_left",
        "rotate_right")

func _physics_process(delta):
    constant_force = thrust
    constant_torque = rotation_dir * spin_power
```

The get_input() function captures the key actions and sets the ship's thrust on or off. Note that the direction of the thrust is based on the body's transform.x, which always represents the body's "forward" direction (see the *Appendix* for an overview of transforms).

Input.get_axis() returns a value based on two inputs, representing negative and positive values. So, rotation_dir will be clockwise, counter-clockwise, or zero, depending on the state of the two input actions.

Finally, when using physics bodies, their movement and related functions should always be called in _physics_process(). Here, you can apply the forces set by the inputs to actually move the body.

Play the scene, and you should be able to fly around freely.

Screen wrap

Another feature of classic 2D arcade games is *screen wrap*. If the player goes off one side of the screen, they appear on the other side. In practice, you teleport the ship to the other side by instantly changing its position. You'll need to know the size of the screen, so add the following variable to the top of the script:

```
var screensize = Vector.ZERO
```

And add this to _ready():

```
screensize = get_viewport_rect().size
```

Later, you can have the game's main script handle setting `screensize` for all the game's objects, but for now, this will allow you to test the screen wrapping with just the player's scene.

When first approaching this problem, you might think you could use the body's `position` property and, if it exceeds the bounds of the screen, set it to the opposite side. And if you were using any other node type, that would work just fine; however, when using `RigidBody2D`, you can't directly set `position` because that would conflict with the movement that the physics engine is calculating. A common mistake is to try adding something like this:

```
func _physics_process(delta):
    if position.x > screensize.x:
        position.x = 0
    if position.x < 0:
        position.x = screensize.x
    if position.y > screensize.y:
        position.y = 0
    if position.y < 0:
        position.y = screensize.y
```

And if you wanted to try this with the `Area2D` in *Coin Dash*, it would work perfectly fine. Here, it will fail, trapping the player on the edge of the screen and glitching unpredictably at the corners. So, what is the answer?

To quote the `RigidBody2D` documentation:

> *Note: You should not change a RigidBody2D's* position *or* linear_velocity *every frame or even very often. If you need to directly affect the body's state, use* _integrate_forces, *which allows you to directly access the physics state.*

And in the description for _integrate_forces():

> *(It) Allows you to read and safely modify the simulation state for the object. Use this instead of* _physics_process *if you need to directly change the body's position or other physics properties.*

So, the answer is to use this separate function when you want to directly affect the rigid body's position. Using `_integrate_forces()` gives you access to the body's `PhysicsDirectBodyState2D` – a Godot object containing a great deal of useful information about the current state of the body. Since you want to change the body's location, that means you need to modify its `Transform2D`.

A **transform** is a matrix representing one or more transformations in space, such as translation, rotation, and/or scaling. The translation (i.e., position) information is found by accessing the `origin` property of the `Transform2D`.

Using this information, you can implement the wrap-around effect by adding the following code:

```
func _integrate_forces(physics_state):
    var xform = physics_state.transform
    xform.origin.x = wrapf(xform.origin.x, 0, screensize.x)
    xform.origin.y = wrapf(xform.origin.y, 0, screensize.y)
    physics_state.transform = xform
```

The `wrapf()` function takes a value (the first argument) and "wraps" it between any min/max values you choose. So, if the value goes below 0, it becomes `screensize.x`, and vice versa.

Note that you're using `physics_state` for the parameter name rather than the default of `state`. This is to avoid confusion since `state` is already being used to track the player's state.

Run the scene again and check that everything is working as expected. Make sure you try wrapping around in all four directions.

Shooting

Now it's time to give your ship some weapons. When pressing the `shoot` action, a bullet/laser should be spawned at the front of the ship and then travel in a straight line until it exits the screen. The player isn't allowed to shoot again until a small amount of time has passed (also known as a **cooldown**).

Bullet scene

This is the node setup for the bullet:

- `Area2D` named `Bullet`

  - `Sprite2D`

  - `CollisionShape2D`

  - `VisibleOnScreenNotifier2D`

Use `res://assets/laser.png` from the assets folder for the **Texture** property of the `Sprite2D` and a `CapsuleShape2D` for the collision shape. You'll need to set **Rotation** of `CollisionShape2D` to 90 so that it is oriented correctly. You should also scale `Sprite2D` down to about half the size: `(0.5, 0.5)`.

Add the following script to the `Bullet` node:

```
extends Area2D

@export var speed = 1000

var velocity = Vector2.ZERO

func start(_transform):
    transform = _transform
    velocity = transform.x * speed

func _process(delta):
    position += velocity * delta
```

You'll call the `start()` function whenever you spawn a new bullet. By passing it a transform, you can give it the correct position *and* rotation – typically that of the ship's gun (more about this later).

The `VisibleOnScreenNotifier2D` is a node that informs you (via a signal) whenever a node becomes visible/invisible. You can use this to automatically delete a bullet that goes offscreen. Connect the node's `screen_exited` signal and add this:

```
func _on_visible_on_screen_notifier_2d_screen_exited():
    queue_free()
```

Finally, connect the bullet's `body_entered` signal so that it can detect when it hits a rock. The bullet doesn't need to know anything about rocks, just that it has hit something. When you create the rock, you'll add it to a group called `rocks` and give it an `explode()` method:

```
func _on_bullet_body_entered(body):
    if body.is_in_group("rocks"):
        body.explode()
        queue_free()
```

Firing bullets

The next step is to create instances of the `Bullet` scene whenever the player presses the `shoot` action. However, if you make the bullet a child of the player, then it will move and rotate along with the player instead of moving independently. You could add the bullet to the main scene using `get_parent()`. `add_child()`, since the `Main` scene will be the parent of the player when the game is running. However, this would mean that you could no longer run and test the `Player` scene by itself. Or, if you decided to rearrange your `Main` scene, making the player a child of some other node, the bullet wouldn't be added where you expect.

In general, it is a bad idea to write code that assumes a fixed tree layout. Especially try to avoid situations where you use get_parent() if at all possible. You may find it difficult to think this way at first, but it will result in a much more modular design and prevent some common mistakes.

In any case, the SceneTree will always exist, and for this game, it will be fine to make the bullet a child of the tree's root, which is the Window containing the game.

Add a Marker2D node to the player and name it Muzzle. This will mark the muzzle of the gun – the location where the bullet will spawn. Set **Position** to (50, 0) to place it directly in front of the ship.

Next, add a Timer node and name it GunCooldown. This will provide a cooldown to the gun, preventing a new bullet from firing until a certain amount of time has passed. Check the **One Shot** and **Autostart** boxes to "on."

Add these new variables to the player's script:

```
@export var bullet_scene : PackedScene
@export var fire_rate = 0.25

var can_shoot = true
```

Drag the bullet.tscn file onto the new **Bullet** property in the Inspector.

Add this line to _ready():

```
$GunCooldown.wait_time = fire_rate
```

And this to get_input():

```
if Input.is_action_pressed("shoot") and can_shoot:
    shoot()
```

Now create the shoot() function, which will handle creating the bullet(s):

```
func shoot():
    if state == INVULNERABLE:
        return
    can_shoot = false
    $GunCooldown.start()
    var b = bullet_scene.instantiate()
    get_tree().root.add_child(b)
    b.start($Muzzle.global_transform)
```

When shooting, you first set can_shoot to false so that the action no longer calls shoot(). Then you add the new bullet as a child of whatever node is the root of the scene tree. Finally, you call the bullet's start() function and give it the muzzle node's *global* transform. Note that if you used transform here, you'd be giving it the muzzle's position relative to the player (which is (50, 0), remember?), and so the bullet would spawn in entirely the wrong place. This is another example of how important it is to understand the distinction between local and global coordinates.

To allow the gun to shoot again, connect the `timeout` signal of `GunCooldown`:

```
func _on_gun_cooldown_timeout():
    can_shoot = true
```

Testing the player's ship

Create a new scene using a `Node` named `Main` and add a `Sprite2D` named `Background` as a child. Use `res://assets/space_background.png` in the **Texture** property. Add an instance of the `Player` to the scene.

Play the main scene and test that you can fly and shoot.

Now that your player's ship works, it's a good time to pause and check your understanding. Working with rigid bodies can be tricky; take a few minutes to experiment with some of the settings and code from this section. Just make sure to change them back before moving on to the next section, where you'll add the asteroids to the game.

Adding the rocks

The goal of the game is to destroy the floating space rocks, so now that you can shoot, it's time to add them. Like the ship, the rocks will use `RigidBody2D`, which will make them travel in a straight line at a steady speed unless disturbed. They'll also bounce off each other in a realistic fashion. To make things more interesting, rocks will start out large and, when you shoot them, break into multiple smaller rocks.

Scene setup

Start a new scene with a `RigidBody2D` node named `Rock`, and add a `Sprite2D` child using the `res://assets/rock.png` texture. Add a `CollisionShape2D`, but *don't* set its shape yet. Because you'll be spawning different-sized rocks, the collision shape will need to be set in code and adjusted to the correct size.

You don't want the rocks coasting to a stop, so they need to ignore the default linear and angular damping. Set both **Linear/Damp** and **Angular/Damp** to 0 and **Damp Mode** for both to *Replace*. The rocks also need to bounce off each other. You can do that in the **Physics Material** property. Select `New PhysicsMaterial` and then click on it to expand. Set the displayed **Bounce** property to 1.

Variable size rocks

Attach a script to Rock and define the member variables:

```
extends RigidBody2D

var screensize = Vector2.ZERO
var size
var radius
var scale_factor = 0.2
```

The Main script will handle spawning new rocks, both at the beginning of a level as well as the smaller rocks that will appear after a large one explodes. A large rock will have a size of 3, break into rocks of size 2, and so on. The scale_factor is multiplied by size to set the Sprite2D scale, the collision radius, and so on. You can adjust this later to change how big each category of rock is.

All of this will be set by the start() method:

```
func start(_position, _velocity, _size):
    position = _position
    size = _size
    mass = 1.5 * size
    $Sprite2D.scale = Vector2.ONE * scale_factor * size
    radius = int($Sprite2D.texture.get_size().x / 2 *
        $Sprite2D.scale.x)
    var shape = CircleShape2D.new()
    shape.radius = radius
    $CollisionShape2d.shape = shape
    linear_velocity = _velocity
    angular_velocity = randf_range(-PI, PI)
```

This is where you calculate the correct collision size based on the rock's size. Note that since position and size are already in use as class variables, you can use an underscore for the function's arguments to prevent conflict.

The rocks also need to wrap around the screen like the player, so use the same technique with _integrate_forces():

```
func _integrate_forces(physics_state):
    var xform = physics_state.transform
    xform.origin.x = wrapf(xform.origin.x, 0 - radius,
        screensize.x + radius)
    xform.origin.y = wrapf(xform.origin.y, 0 - radius,
        screensize.y + radius)
    physics_state.transform = xform
```

The one difference here is that including the rock's `radius` in the calculation results in smoother-looking teleportation. The rock will appear to fully exit the screen before entering the opposite side. You may want to do the same thing with the player's ship. Try it and see which you like better.

Instantiating rocks

When new rocks are spawned, the main scene will need to pick a random starting location. To do this, you could use some math to pick a random point along the perimeter of the screen, but instead, you can take advantage of another Godot node type. You'll draw a path around the edge of the screen, and the script will pick a random location along that path.

In the `Main` scene, add a `Path2D` node and name it `RockPath`. When you select the node, you will see some new buttons appear at the top of the editor window:

Figure 3.9: Path drawing tools

Select the middle one (**Add Point**) to draw the path by clicking the points shown in the following screenshot. To make the points align, make sure **Use Grid Snap** is checked. This option is found in the icon bar at the top of the editor window:

Figure 3.10: Enabling grid snapping

Draw the points in the order shown in the following screenshot. After clicking the fourth point, click the **Close Curve** button (marked 5 in the screenshot) and your path will be complete:

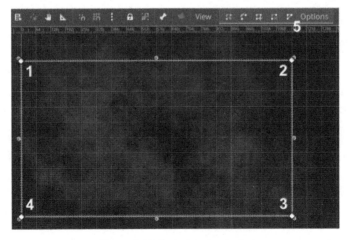

Figure 3.11: Path drawing order

Don't click in the editor window again if you have `RockPath` selected! If you do, you'll add additional points to the curve, and your rocks may not spawn where you want them to. You can press *Ctrl + Z* to undo any extra points you may have added.

Now that the path is defined, add a `PathFollow2D` as a child of `RockPath` and name it `RockSpawn`. This node's purpose is to automatically move along its parent path using its **Progress** property, which represents an offset along the path. The higher the offset, the further along the path it goes. Since our path is closed, it will also loop if the offset value is bigger than the path's length.

Add the following script to `Main.gd`:

```
extends Node

@export var rock_scene : PackedScene

var screensize = Vector2.ZERO

func _ready():
    screensize = get_viewport().get_visible_rect().size
    for i in 3:
        spawn_rock(3)
```

You start by getting the `screensize` so that you can pass it to the rocks when they're spawned. Then, you spawn three rocks of size 3. Don't forget to drag `rock.tscn` onto the **Rock** property.

Here is the `spawn_rock()` function:

```
func spawn_rock(size, pos=null, vel=null):
    if pos == null:
        $RockPath/RockSpawn.progress = randi()
        pos = $RockPath/RockSpawn.position
    if vel == null:
        vel = Vector2.RIGHT.rotated(randf_range(0, TAU)) *
            randf_range(50, 125)
    var r = rock_scene.instantiate()
    r.screensize = screensize
    r.start(pos, vel, size)
    call_deferred("add_child", r)
```

This function serves two purposes. When called with only a `size` parameter, it picks a random position along the `RockPath` and a random velocity. However, if those values are provided, it will use them instead. This will let you spawn the smaller rocks at the location of the explosion by specifying their properties.

Run the game and you should see three rocks floating around, but your bullets don't affect them.

Exploding rocks

The bullet checks for bodies in the `rocks` group, so in the `Rock` scene, select the **Node** tab and choose **Groups**. Type `rocks` and click **Add**:

Figure 3.12: Adding a "rocks" group

Now, if you run the game and shoot a rock, you'll see an error message because the bullet is trying to call the rock's `explode()` method, which you haven't defined yet. This method needs to do three things:

- Remove the rock
- Play an explosion animation
- Notify `Main` to spawn new, smaller rocks

Explosion scene

The explosion will be a separate scene, which you can add to the `Rock` and later to the `Player`. It will contain two nodes:

- `Sprite2D` named `Explosion`
- `AnimationPlayer`

For the `Sprite2D` node's **Texture** property, use `res://assets/explosion.png`. You'll notice this is a **sprite sheet** – an image made up of 64 smaller images laid out in a grid pattern. These images are the individual frames of the animation. You'll often find animations packaged this way, and Godot's `Sprite2D` node supports using them.

In the Inspector, find the sprite's **Animation** section. Set **Vframes** and **Hframes** both to 8. This will slice the sprite sheet into its 64 individual images. You can verify this by changing the **Frame** property to different values between 0 and 63. Make sure to set it back to 0 before you continue.

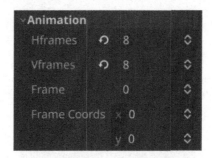

Figure 3.13: Sprite Animation settings

The `AnimationPlayer` node can be used to animate any property of any node. You'll use it to change the **Frame** property over time. Start by selecting the node and you'll see the **Animation** panel open at the bottom:

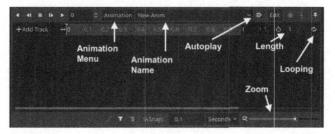

Figure 3.14: Animation panel

Click the **Animation** button and choose **New**. Name the animation `explosion`. Set **Animation Length** to `0.64` and **Snap** to `0.01`. Select the `Sprite2D` node and you'll notice that each property in the Inspector now has a key symbol next to it. Clicking on a key will create a *keyframe* in the current animation.

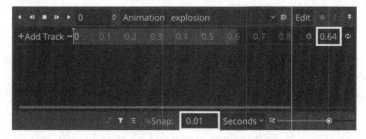

Figure 3.15: Animation time settings

Click the key next to the `Explosion` node's **Frame** property and confirm that you want to create a new animation track. Deselect **Create RESET Track(s)**. You've now created a keyframe telling the `AnimationPlayer` that at time 0, you want the sprite's **Frame** to be 0.

Slide the scrubber to time 0.64 (you can adjust the zoom using the slider if you can't see it). Set **Frame** to 63 and click the key again. Now the animation knows to use the last image at the animation's final time. However, you also need to let the AnimationPlayer know that you want to use all the intermediate values in the times between those two points. At the right side of the animation track is an **Update Mode** dropdown. It's currently set to **Discrete**, and you need to change it to **Continuous**:

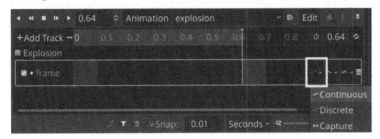

Figure 3.16: Setting Update Mode

Click the **Play** button in the **Animation** panel to see the animation.

You can now add the explosion to the rock. In the Rock scene, add an instance of Explosion and click the eye icon next to the node to make it hidden. Add this line to start():

```
$Explosion.scale = Vector2.ONE * 0.75 * size
```

This will ensure the explosion is scaled to match the rock's size.

Add a signal called exploded at the top of the script, then add the explode() function, which will be called when the bullet hits the rock:

```
func explode():
    $CollisionShape2D.set_deferred("disabled", true)
    $Sprite2d.hide()
    $Explosion/AnimationPlayer.play("explosion")
    $Explosion.show()
    exploded.emit(size, radius, position, linear_velocity)
    linear_velocity = Vector2.ZERO
    angular_velocity = 0
    await $Explosion/AnimationPlayer.animation_finished
    queue_free()
```

Here, you hide the rock and play the explosion, waiting for it to finish before removing the rock. When you emit the exploded signal, you also include all the rock's information, so that spawn_rock() in Main will be able to spawn the smaller rocks at the same location.

Test the game and check that you can see explosions when you shoot the rocks.

Spawning smaller rocks

The Rock scene is emitting the signal, but Main isn't listening for it yet. You can't connect the signal in the **Node** tab because the rocks are being instanced in the code. They won't exist until later, when the game is running. Add this line to the end of spawn_rock():

```
r.exploded.connect(self._on_rock_exploded)
```

This connects the rock's signal to a function in Main, which you also need to create:

```
func _on_rock_exploded(size, radius, pos, vel):
    if size <= 1:
        return
    for offset in [-1, 1]:
        var dir = $Player.position.direction_to(pos)
            .orthogonal() * offset
        var newpos = pos + dir * radius
        var newvel = dir * vel.length() * 1.1
        spawn_rock(size - 1, newpos, newvel)
```

In this function, you create two new rocks unless the rock that was just destroyed was of size 1 (the smallest size). The offset loop variable ensures that the two new rocks travel in opposite directions (that is, one's velocity will be negative). The dir variable finds the vector between the player and the rock, then uses orthogonal() to get a vector that's perpendicular. This ensures that the new rocks don't fly straight toward the player.

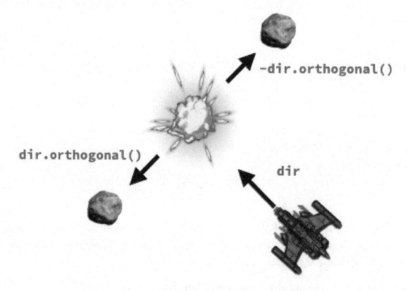

Figure 3.17: Explosion diagram

Play the game once again and check that everything is working as expected.

This is a good place to stop and review what you've done so far. You've completed all the basic functionality of the game: the player can fly around and shoot; the rocks float, bounce, and explode; and new rocks are spawned. You should be feeling more comfortable using rigid bodies at this point. In the next section, you'll start building the interface to allow the player to start the game and see important information during gameplay.

Creating the UI

Creating a UI for your game can be very complex, or at least time-consuming. Precisely placing individual elements and ensuring they work across different-sized screens and devices is the least interesting part of game development for many programmers. Godot provides a wide variety of `Control` nodes to assist in this process. Learning how to use the various `Control` nodes will help lessen the pain of creating a polished UI.

For this game, you don't need a very complex UI. The game needs to provide the following information and interactions:

- Start button
- Status message (such as "Get Ready" or "Game Over")
- Score
- Lives counter

Here is a preview of what you will make:

Figure 3.18: UI layout

Create a new scene and add a `CanvasLayer` node with the name HUD as the root node. You'll build the UI on this layer using the `Control` node's layout features.

Layout

Godot's Control nodes include a number of specialized containers. These nodes can be nested inside each other to create the exact layout you need. For example, a MarginContainer automatically adds padding around its contents, while HBoxContainer and VBoxContainer organize their contents in rows or columns, respectively.

Follow these steps to build the layout:

1. Start by adding Timer and MarginContainer children, which will hold the score and life counters. In the **Layout** dropdown, select **Top Wide**.

Figure 3.19: Top Wide control alignment

2. In the Inspector, set the four margins in **Theme Overrides/Constants** to 20.

3. Set the **One Shot** property of Timer to on and its **Wait Time** to 2.

4. As a child of the container, add an HBoxContainer, which will position the score counter on the left and the lives counter on the right. Under this container, add a Label (name it ScoreLabel) and another HBoxContainer (named LivesCounter).

   Set the ScoreLabel's **Text** to 0, and under **Layout/Container Sizing/Horizontal**, check the **Expand** box. In **Label Settings**, add a font as you did in *Chapter 2*, using res://assets/kenvector_future_thin.ttf and setting the font size to 64.

5. Select LivesCounter and set **Theme Overrides/Constants/Separation** to 20, then add a child TextureRect and name it L1. Drag res://assets/player_small.png to the **Texture** property and set **Stretch Mode** to **Keep Aspect Centered**. Make sure you have the L1 node selected and press *duplicate* (*Ctrl + D*) twice to create L2 and L3 (they'll be named automatically). During the game, the HUD will show or hide these three textures to indicate how many lives the player has left.

6. In a larger, more complex UI, you might save this section as its own scene and embed it in other section(s) of the UI. However, this game only needs a few more elements, so it's fine to combine them all in one scene.

7. As a child of HUD, add a VBoxContainer, and inside it, add a Label named Message and a TextureButton named StartButton. Set the layout of the VBoxContainer to **Center Wide** and **Theme Overrides/ Constants/ Separation** to 100.

8. In the res://assets folder, there are two textures for StartButton, one normal (play_button.png) and one to show when the mouse is hovering over it ('play_button_h.png). Drag these to **Textures/Normal** and **Textures/Hover** in the Inspector. Set the button's **Layout/Container Sizing/Horizontal** to **Shrink Center** so that it will be centered horizontally.

9. Set the Message text to "Space Rocks!" and set its font using the same settings as ScoreLabel. Set **Horizontal Alignment** to **Center**.

When finished, your scene tree should look like this:

Figure 3.20: HUD node layout

Scripting the UI

You've completed the UI layout, now add a script to HUD. Since the nodes you'll need to reference are located under containers, you can store references to them in variables at the start. Since this needs to happen after nodes are added to the tree, you can use the @onready decorator to cause the variable's value to be set at the same time as the _ready() function runs.

```
extends CanvasLayer

signal start_game
```

```
@onready var lives_counter = $MarginContainer/HBoxContainer/
LivesCounter.get_children()
@onready var score_label = $MarginContainer/HBoxContainer/ScoreLabel
@onready var message = $VBoxContainer/Message
@onready var start_button = $VBoxContainer/StartButton
```

You'll emit the start_game signal when the player clicks the StartButton. The lives_counter variable is an array holding references to the three life-counter images so they can be hidden/shown as needed.

Next, you need functions to handle updating the displayed information:

```
func show_message(text):
    message.text = text
    message.show()
    $Timer.start()

func update_score(value):
    score_label.text = str(value)

func update_lives(value):
    for item in 3:
        lives_counter[item].visible = value > item
```

Main will call these functions whenever the relevant value changes. Now add a function to handle the end of the game:

```
func game_over():
    show_message("Game Over")
    await $Timer.timeout
    start_button.show()
```

Connect the pressed signal of StartButton and the timeout signal of Timer:

```
func _on_start_button_pressed():
    start_button.hide()
    start_game.emit()

func _on_timer_timeout():
    message.hide()
    message.text = ""
```

The Main scene's UI code

Add an instance of the HUD scene to the Main scene. Add these variables to main.gd:

```
var level = 0
var score = 0
var playing = false
```

And a function to handle starting a new game:

```
func new_game():
    # remove any old rocks from previous game
    get_tree().call_group("rocks", "queue_free")
    level = 0
    score = 0
    $HUD.update_score(score)
    $HUD.show_message("Get Ready!")
    $Player.reset()
    await $HUD/Timer.timeout
    playing = true
```

Note the $Player.reset() line – don't worry, you'll add that soon.

When the player destroys all the rocks, they'll advance to the next level:

```
func new_level():
    level += 1
    $HUD.show_message("Wave %s" % level)
    for i in level:
        spawn_rock(3)
```

You'll call this function every time the level changes. It announces the level number and spawns a number of rocks to match. Note that since you initialized level to 0, this will set it to 1 for the first level. You should also remove the code that's spawning rocks in _ready() – you don't need that anymore.

To detect when the level has ended, you need to check how many rocks are left:

```
func _process(delta):
    if not playing:
        return
    if get_tree().get_nodes_in_group("rocks").size() == 0:
        new_level()
```

Next, you need to connect the HUD's start_game signal to the new_game() function of Main.

Select the HUD instance in `Main` and find its `start_game` signal in the **Node** tab. Click **Connect**, but in the popup, click the **Pick** button next to **Receiver Method**. You'll see a list of the functions in `Main`, and you can select the `new_game()` function:

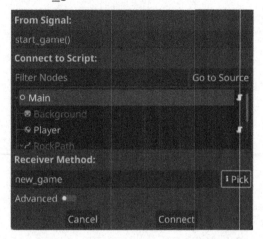

Figure 3.21: Connecting a signal to an existing function

Add this function to handle what happens when the game ends:

```
func game_over():
    playing = false
    $HUD.game_over()
```

Player code

Add the new signals and a new variable to `player.gd`:

```
signal lives_changed
signal dead

var reset_pos = false
var lives = 0: set = set_lives

func set_lives(value):
    lives = value
    lives_changed.emit(lives)
    if lives <= 0:
        change_state(DEAD)
    else:
        change_state(INVULNERABLE)
```

For the `lives` variable, you've added something called a **setter**. This means that whenever the value of `lives` changes, the `set_lives()` function will be called. This lets you automatically emit the signal as well as checking when it reaches `0`.

The `reset()` function is called by `Main` when a new game starts:

```
func reset():
    reset_pos = true
    $Sprite2d.show()
    lives = 3
    change_state(ALIVE)
```

Resetting the player means setting its position back to the center of the screen. As we saw before, that needs to be done in `_integrate_forces()` in order to work. Add this to that function:

```
if reset_pos:
    physics_state.transform.origin = screensize / 2
    reset_pos = false
```

Back in the `Main` scene, select the `Player` instance and find its `lives_changed` signal in the **Node** tab. Click **Connect**, and under **Connect to Script**, choose the HUD node and type `update_lives` in **Receiver Method**.

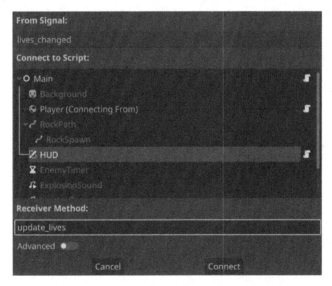

Figure 3.22: Connecting the player signal to HUD

In this section, you made a much more complex UI than in previous projects, including some new `Control` nodes such as `TextureProgressBar`, and used signals to connect everything together. In the next section, you'll handle the end of the game: what should happen when the player dies.

Ending the game

In this section, you'll make the player detect when it is hit by rocks, add an invulnerability feature, and end the game when the player runs out of lives.

Add an instance of the `Explosion` scene to the `Player` scene and uncheck its **Visibility** property. Also add a `Timer` node named `InvulnerabilityTimer` and set **Wait Time** to 2 and **One Shot** to "on."

You'll emit the `dead` signal to notify `Main` that the game should end. Before that, however, you need to update the state machine to do a little more with each state:

```
func change_state(new_state):
    match new_state:
        INIT:
            $CollisionShape2D.set_deferred("disabled",
                true)
            $Sprite2D.modulate.a = 0.5
        ALIVE:
            $CollisionShape2d.set_deferred("disabled",
                false)
            $Sprite2d.modulate.a = 1.0
        INVULNERABLE:
            $CollisionShape2d.set_deferred("disabled",
                true)
            $Sprite2d.modulate.a = 0.5
            $InvulnerabilityTimer.start()
        DEAD:
            $CollisionShape2d.set_deferred("disabled",
                true)
            $Sprite2d.hide()
            linear_velocity = Vector2.ZERO
            dead.emit()
    state = new_state
```

The `modulate.a` property of a sprite sets its alpha channel (transparency). Setting it to `0.5` makes it semi-transparent, while `1.0` is solid.

After entering the `INVULNERABLE` state, you start the timer. Connect its `timeout` signal:

```
func _on_invulnerability_timer_timeout():
    change_state(ALIVE)
```

Detecting collisions between rigid bodies

When you fly around, the ship bounces off rocks because both are rigid bodies. However, if you want to make something happen when two rigid bodies collide, you need to enable **contact monitoring**. In the `Player` scene, select the `Player` node, and in the Inspector, set **Contact Monitor** to on. By default, no contacts are reported, so set **Max Contacts Reported** to 1. Now the player will emit a signal when it comes into contact with another body. Click on the **Node** tab and connect the `body_entered` signal:

```
func _on_body_entered(body):
    if body.is_in_group("rocks"):
        body.explode()
        lives -= 1
        explode()

func explode():
    $Explosion.show()
    $Explosion/AnimationPlayer.play("explosion")
    await $Explosion/AnimationPlayer.animation_finished
    $Explosion.hide()
```

Now go to the `Main` scene and connect the `Player` instance's `dead` signal to the `game_over()` method. Play the game and try running into a rock. Your ship should explode, become invulnerable for two seconds, and lose one life. Also check that the game ends if you get hit three times.

In this section, you learned about rigid body collisions and used them to handle the ship colliding with rocks. The full game cycle is now complete: the start screen leads to gameplay, which ends with a game over display. In the remaining sections of the chapter, you'll add some additional features to the game, such as a pause function.

Pausing the game

Many games require some sort of pause mode to allow the player to take a break from the action. In Godot, pausing is a function of the `SceneTree` and can be set using its `paused` property. When the `SceneTree` is paused, three things happen:

- The physics thread stops running

- `_process()` and `_physics_process()` are no longer called on any nodes

- The `_input()` and `_input_event()` methods are also not called for inputs

When pause mode is triggered, every node in the running game reacts accordingly, based on how you've configured it. This behavior is set via the node's **Process/Mode** property, which you'll find near the bottom of the Inspector list.

The pause mode can be set to the following values:

- `Inherit` – The node uses the same mode as its parent

- `Pausable` – The node pauses when the scene tree is paused

- `When Paused` – The node only runs when the tree is paused

- `Always` – The node always runs, ignoring the tree's paused state

- `Disabled` – The node never runs, ignoring the tree's paused state

Open the **Input Map** tab and create a new input action called `pause`. Assign a key you'd like to use to toggle pause mode. `P` is a good choice.

Add the following function to `Main.gd`:

```
func _input(event):
    if event.is_action_pressed("pause"):
        if not playing:
            return
        get_tree().paused = not get_tree().paused
        var message = $HUD/VBoxContainer/Message
        if get_tree().paused:
            message.text = "Paused"
            message.show()
        else:
            message.text = ""
            message.hide()
```

This code detects pressing the key and toggles the tree's `paused` state to the opposite of its current state. It also displays **Paused** on the screen so that it doesn't just appear that the game has frozen.

If you were to run the game now, you'd have a problem – all nodes are paused, including `Main`. That means it's not processing `_input()` anymore, so it can't detect the input again to unpause the game! To fix this, set **Process/Mode** of the `Main` node to **Always**.

The pause function is a very useful one to know about. You can use this technique in any game you make, so review it to make sure you understand how it works. You can even try going back and adding it to *Coin Dash*. Our next section adds to the action by adding enemies to the game.

Enemies

Space is filled with more dangers than just rocks. In this section, you'll create an enemy spaceship that will periodically appear and shoot at the player.

Following a path

When the enemy appears, it should follow a path across the screen. It'll also look better if it's not just a straight line. To keep it from looking too repetitive, you can create multiple paths and randomly choose one when the enemy appears.

Create a new scene and add a Node. Name it EnemyPaths and save it. To draw the path, add a Path2D node. As you saw earlier, this node allows you to draw a series of connected points. Selecting this node displays a new menu bar:

Figure 3.23: Path drawing options

These buttons let you draw and modify the path's points. Click the one with the green + symbol to add points. Click to start the path somewhere just outside the game window, and then click a few more points to make a curve. Note that the arrows indicate the direction of the path. Don't worry about making it smooth yet:

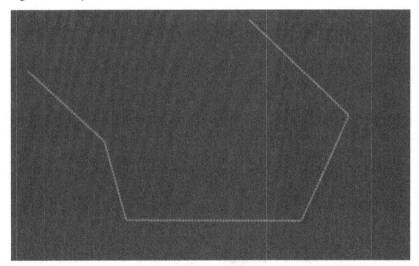

Figure 3.24: An example path

When the enemy follows the path, it will not look very smooth when it hits the sharp corners. To smooth the curve, click the second button in the path toolbar (its tooltip says **Select Control Points**). Now, if you click and drag any of the curve's points, you will add a control point that allows you to curve the line at that point. Smoothing the line above results in something like this:

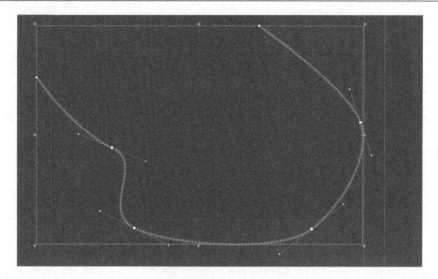

Figure 3.25: Using control points

Add two or three more `Path2D` nodes to the scene and draw the paths however you like. Adding loops and curves rather than straight lines will make the enemy look more dynamic (and make it harder to hit). Remember that the first point you click will be the start of the path, so make sure to start them on different sides of the screen for variety. Here are three example paths:

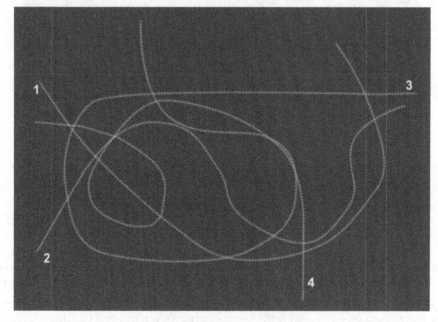

Figure 3.26: Adding multiple paths

Save the scene. You'll add this to the enemy's scene to give it the paths it can follow.

Enemy scene

Create a new scene for the enemy, using an `Area2D` as its root node. Add a `Sprite2D` child and use `res://assets/enemy_saucer.png` as its **Texture** property. Set **Animation/HFrames** to 3 so that you can choose between the different colored saucers:

1. As you've done before, add a `CollisionShape2D` and give it a `CircleShape2D` scaled to cover the image. Add an instance of the `EnemyPaths` scene and an `AnimationPlayer`. In the `AnimationPlayer`, you'll add an animation to create a flash effect when the saucer is hit.

2. Add an animation named `flash`. Set **Length** to `0.25` and **Snap** to `0.01`. The property you'll be animating is the `Sprite2D`'s **Modulate** property (found under **Visibility**). Add a keyframe for **Modulate** to create the track, then move the scrubber to `0.04` and change the **Modulate** color to red. Move forward another `0.04` and change the color back to white.

3. Repeat this process two more times so that you have three flashes in total.

4. Add an instance of the `Explosion` scene and hide it. Add a `Timer` node named GunCooldown to control how often the enemy will shoot. Set **Wait Time** to `1.5` and **Autostart** to on.

5. Add a script to the enemy and connect the timer's `timeout`. Don't add anything to the function yet.

6. In the **Node** tab of Area2D, add it to a group called `enemies`. As with the rocks, this will give you a way to identify the object, even if there are multiple enemies on the screen at the same time.

Moving the enemy

To begin, you'll write the code to select a path and move the enemy along it:

```
extends Area2D

@export var bullet_scene : PackedScene
@export var speed = 150
@export var rotation_speed = 120
@export var health = 3

var follow = PathFollow2D.new()
var target = null

func _ready():
    $Sprite2D.frame = randi() % 3
    var path = $EnemyPaths.get_children()[randi() %
        $EnemyPaths.get_child_count()]
```

```
    path.add_child(follow)
    follow.loop = false
```

Recall that the `PathFollow2D` node automatically moves along a parent `Path2D`. By default, it loops around the path when it reaches the end, so you need to set that to `false` to disable it.

The next step is to move along the path and remove the enemy when it reaches the end of the path:

```
func _physics_process(delta):
    rotation += deg_to_rad(rotation_speed) * delta
    follow.progress += speed * delta
    position = follow.global_position
    if follow.progress_ratio >= 1:
        queue_free()
```

You can detect the end of the path when `progress` is greater than the total path length. However, it's more straightforward to use `progress_ratio`, which varies from zero to one over the length of the path, so you don't need to know how long each path is.

Spawning enemies

In the `Main` scene, add a new `Timer` node called `EnemyTimer`. Set its **One Shot** property to on. Then, in `main.gd`, add a variable to reference the enemy scene:

```
@export var enemy_scene : PackedScene
```

Add this line to `new_level()`:

```
$EnemyTimer.start(randf_range(5, 10))
```

Connect the `EnemyTimer`'s `timeout` signal:

```
func _on_enemy_timer_timeout():
    var e = enemy_scene.instantiate()
    add_child(e)
    e.target = $Player
    $EnemyTimer.start(randf_range(20, 40))
```

This code instances the enemy whenever `EnemyTimer` times out. You don't want another enemy for a while, so the timer is restarted with a longer delay.

Play the game, and you should see a saucer appear and fly along its path.

Shooting and collisions

The enemy needs to shoot at the player as well as react when hit by the player or the player's bullets.

The enemy's bullet will be similar to the player's, but we'll use a different texture. You can create it again from scratch or use the following process to reuse the node setup.

Open the `Bullet` scene and choose **Scene** | **Save Scene As** to save it as `enemy_bullet.tscn` (afterward, don't forget to rename the root node as well). Remove the script by clicking the **Detach the script** button. Disconnect the signal connections by clicking the **Node** tab and choosing **Disconnect**. You can see which nodes have their signals connected by looking for the 🔝 icon next to the node name.

Replace the sprite's texture with the `laser_green.png` image, and add a new script to the root node.

The script for the enemy bullet will be very similar to the regular bullet. Connect the area's `body_entered` signal and the `screen_exited` signal of `VisibleOnScreenNotifier2D`:

```
extends Area2D

@export var speed = 1000

func start(_pos, _dir):
    position = _pos
    rotation = _dir.angle()

func _process(delta):
    position += transform.x * speed * delta

func _on_body_entered(body):
    queue_free()

func _on_visible_on_screen_notifier_2d_screen_exited():
    queue_free()
```

Note that you'll need to specify a position and direction for the bullet. That's because, unlike the player, who always shoots forward, the enemy will always shoot toward the player.

For now, the bullet won't do any damage to the player. You'll be adding a shield to the player in the next section, so you can add it at that time.

Save the scene and drag it into the **Bullet** property of the Enemy.

In `enemy.gd`, add a variable for some random variation to the bullet, and the `shoot()` function:

```
@export var bullet_spread = 0.2

func shoot():
    var dir =
        global_position.direction_to(target.global_position)
    dir = dir.rotated(randf_range(-bullet_spread,
```

```
                bullet_spread))
        var b = bullet_scene.instantiate()
        get_tree().root.add_child(b)
        b.start(global_position, dir)
```

First, you find the vector pointing to the player's position, then add a little bit of randomness so that it can "miss."

Call the shoot() function whenever GunCooldown times out:

```
func _on_gun_cooldown_timeout():
    shoot()
```

For an extra challenge, you can make the enemy shoot in pulses or multiple rapid shots:

```
func shoot_pulse(n, delay):
    for i in n:
        shoot()
        await get_tree().create_timer(delay).timeout
```

This will shoot a given number of bullets, n, with delay seconds between them. You can call this instead when the cooldown triggers:

```
func _on_gun_cooldown_timeout():
    shoot_pulse(3, 0.15)
```

This will shoot a pulse of 3 bullets with 0.15 seconds between them. Tough to dodge!

Next, the enemy needs to take damage when it's hit by a shot from the player. It will flash using the animation you made and then explode when its health reaches 0.

Add these functions to enemy.gd:

```
func take_damage(amount):
    health -= amount
    $AnimationPlayer.play("flash")
    if health <= 0:
        explode()

func explode():
    speed = 0
    $GunCooldown.stop()
    $CollisionShape2D.set_deferred("disabled", true)
    $Sprite2D.hide()
    $Explosion.show()
    $Explosion/AnimationPlayer.play("explosion")
```

```
    await $Explosion/AnimationPlayer.animation_finished
    queue_free()
```

Also, connect the enemy's `body_entered` signal so that the enemy will explode if the player runs into it:

```
func _on_body_entered(body):
    if body.is_in_group("rocks"):
        return
    explode()
```

Again, you're waiting for the player shield to be implemented before doing damage to the player, so for now, this collision only destroys the enemy.

Currently, the player's bullet is only detecting rocks because its `body_entered` signal isn't triggered by the enemy, which is an `Area2D`. To detect the enemy, go to the `Bullet` scene and connect the `area_entered` signal:

```
func _on_area_entered(area):
    if area.is_in_group("enemies"):
        area.take_damage(1)
```

Try playing the game again and you'll be doing battle with an aggressive alien opponent! Verify that all the collision combinations are being handled (except for the enemy shooting the player). Also note that the enemy's bullets can be blocked by rocks – maybe you can hide behind them for cover!

Now that the game has enemies, it's a lot more challenging. If you still find it too easy, try increasing the enemy's properties: how often it appears, how much damage it does, and how many shots it takes to destroy it. It's OK if you make it too hard because, in the next section, you'll give the player a little help by adding a shield to absorb damage.

Player shield

In this section, you'll add a shield to the player and a display element to the HUD showing the current shield level.

First, add the following to the top of the `player.gd` script:

```
signal shield_changed

@export var max_shield = 100.0
@export var shield_regen = 5.0

var shield = 0: set = set_shield
```

```
func set_shield(value):
    value = min(value, max_shield)
    shield = value
    shield_changed.emit(shield / max_shield)
    if shield <= 0:
        lives -= 1
        explode()
```

The `shield` variable works similarly to `lives`, emitting a signal whenever it changes. Since the value will be added to by the shield's regeneration, you need to make sure it doesn't go above the `max_shield` value. Then, when you emit the `shield_changed` signal, you pass the ratio of `shield` / `max_shield` rather than the actual value. This way, the HUD's display doesn't need to know anything about how big the shield actually is, just its percentage.

You should also remove the `explode()` line from `_on_body_entered()`, since you now don't want just hitting a rock to blow up the ship – that will now only happen when the shield runs out.

Hitting a rock will damage the shield, and bigger rocks should do more damage:

```
func _on_body_entered(body):
    if body.is_in_group("rocks"):
        shield -= body.size * 25
        body.explode()
```

The enemy's bullets should also do damage, so make this change to `enemy_bullet.gd`:

```
@export var damage = 15

func _on_body_entered(body):
    if body.name == "Player":
        body.shield -= damage
    queue_free()
```

Also, running into the enemy should damage the player, so update this in `enemy.gd`:

```
func _on_body_entered(body):
    if body.is_in_group("rocks"):
        return
    explode()
    body.shield -= 50
```

If the player's shield runs out and they lose a life, you should reset the shield to its maximum. Add this line to `set_lives()`:

```
shield = max_shield
```

The last addition to the player script is to regenerate the shield each frame. Add this line to _process() in player.gd:

```
shield += shield_regen * delta
```

Now that the code is complete, you need to add a new display element to the HUD scene. Rather than display the shield's value as a number, you'll make a **progress bar**. TextureProgressBar is a Control node that displays a given value as a filled bar. It also allows you to assign a texture to be used for the bar.

Go to the HUD scene and add two new nodes as children of the existing HBoxContainer: TextureRect and TextureProgressBar. Rename TextureProgressBar to ShieldBar. Place them after the Score label and before LivesCounter. Your node setup should look like this:

Figure 3.27: Updated HUD node layout

Drag res://assets/shield_gold.png into the **Texture** property of TextureRect. This will be an icon indicating that this bar shows the shield value. Change **Stretch Mode** to **Keep Centered** so that the texture won't be distorted.

The ShieldBar has three **Texture** properties: **Under**, **Over**, and **Progress**. **Progress** is the texture that will be used for the bar's value. Drag res://assets/bar_green_200.png into this property. The other two texture properties let you customize the appearance by setting an image to be drawn above or below the progress texture. Drag res://assets/bar_glass_200.png into the **Over** property.

In the **Range** section, you can set the numerical properties of the bar. **Min Value** and **Max Value** should be set to 0 and 1, as this bar will show the ratio of the shield to its maximum, not its numerical value. This means **Step** must also be smaller – set it to 0.01. **Value** is the property that controls how much of the bar should be "full." Change it to .75 to see the bar partly filled. Also, in the **Layout/Container Sizing** section, check the **Expand** box and set **Vertical** to **Shrink Center**.

The HUD should look like this when you're done:

Figure 3.28: Updated HUD with shield bar

You can now update the script to set the value of the shield bar, as well as to make it change color as it gets closer to zero. Add these variables to hud.gd:

```
@onready var shield_bar =
    $MarginContainer/HBoxContainer/ShieldBar

var bar_textures = {
    "green": preload("res://assets/bar_green_200.png"),
    "yellow": preload("res://assets/bar_yellow_200.png"),
    "red": preload("res://assets/bar_red_200.png")
}
```

In addition to the green bar, you also have red and yellow bars in the assets folder. This allows you to change the shield bar's color as the value decreases. Loading the textures in this way makes them easier to access later in the script when you want to assign the appropriate image to the bar:

```
func update_shield(value):
    shield_bar.texture_progress = bar_textures["green"]
    if value < 0.4:
        shield_bar.texture_progress = bar_textures["red"]
    elif value < 0.7:
        shield_bar.texture_progress = bar_textures["yellow"]
    shield_bar.value = value
```

Finally, click on the Main scene's Player node and connect the shield_changed signal to the HUD's update_shield() function.

Run the game and verify that the shield is working. You may want to increase or decrease the shield regeneration rate to give it a speed you're happy with. When you're ready to move on, in the next section, you'll add some sound to the game.

Sound and visual effects

The structure and gameplay of the game is complete. In this section, you'll add some additional effects to the game to improve the game experience.

Sound and music

In the `res://assets/sounds` folder are several audio effects for the game. To play a sound, it needs to be loaded by an `AudioStreamPlayer` node. Add two of these nodes to the `Player` scene, naming them `LaserSound` and `EngineSound`. Drag the respective sound files into each node's **Stream** property in the Inspector. To play the sound when shooting, add this line to `shoot()` in `player.gd`:

```
$LaserSound.play()
```

Play the game and try shooting. If you find the sound too loud, you can adjust the **Volume dB** property. Try a value of `-10` to start.

The engine sounds works a little differently. It needs to play when the thrust is on, but if you just try to call `play()` on the sound in the `get_input()` function when the player presses the key, it will restart the sound every frame. This doesn't sound good, so you only want to start playing the sound if it isn't already playing. Here is the relevant section of the `get_input()` function:

```
if Input.is_action_pressed("thrust"):
    thrust = transform.x * engine_power
    if not $EngineSound.playing:
        $EngineSound.play()
else:
    $EngineSound.stop()
```

Note that a problem can occur: if the player dies while holding down the thrust key, the engine sound will remain stuck playing because, in the **DEAD** state, you ignore player input. This can be solved by adding `$EngineSound.stop()` to the **DEAD** state in `change_state()`.

In the `Main` scene, add three more `AudioStreamPlayer` nodes: `ExplosionSound`, `LevelupSound`, and `Music`. In their **Stream** properties, drop `explosion.wav`, `levelup.ogg`, and `Funky-Gameplay_Looping.ogg`.

Add `$ExplosionSound.play()` as the first line of `_on_rock_exploded()`, and add `$LevelupSound.play()` to `new_level()`.

To start and stop the background music, add `$Music.play()` to `new_game()` and `$Music.stop()` to `game_over()`.

The enemy also needs `ExplosionSound` and `ShootSound` nodes. You can use `enemy_laser.wav` for their shooting sound.

Particles

The player ship's thrust is a perfect use of particle effects, creating a streaming flame from the engine.

Add a `CPUParticles2D` node and name it `Exhaust`. You might want to zoom in on the ship while you're doing this part.

> **Particle node types**
>
> Godot offers two types of particle nodes: one that uses the CPU and one that uses the GPU for rendering. Since not all platforms, especially mobile or older desktops, support hardware acceleration for particles, you can use the CPU version for wider compatibility. If you know your game will be running on more powerful systems, you can use the GPU version.

You'll see a line of white dots streaming down from the center of the ship. Your challenge now is to turn those dots into an exhaust flame.

There are a very large number of properties to choose from when configuring particles. As you go through the process of setting up this effect, feel free to experiment with them to see how they affect the result.

Set these properties of the `Exhaust` node:

- **Amount**: 25
- **Drawing/Local Coords**: On
- **Transform/Position**: (-28, 0)
- **Transform/Rotation**: 180
- **Visibility/Show Behind Parent**: On

The remaining properties you'll change will affect the behavior of the particles. Start with **Emission Shape**: change it to **Rectangle**. This will reveal **Rect Extents**, which you can set to (1, 5). The particles are now emitted over a small area instead of a single point.

Next, set **Direction/Spread** to 0 and **Gravity** to (0, 0). Note that the particles are not falling or spreading out, although they are moving very slowly.

Set **Initial Velocity/Velocity Max** to 400, then scroll down to **Scale/Scale Amount Max** and set it to 8.

To make the size change over time, you can set **Scale Amount Curve**. Select **New Curve** and then click to open it. In the small graph that shows, right-click to add two points – one on the left and one on the right. Drag the right-hand dot down until the curve looks like this:

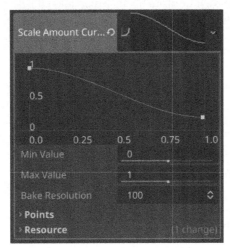

Figure 3.29: Adding a particle scale curve

You should now see the particles shrinking as they stream out from the back of the ship.

The last section to adjust is **Color**. To make the particles appear like a flame, they should start out bright orange-yellow and shift to red as they fade out. In the **Color Ramp** property, click on **New Gradient**, and you'll see a gradient editor that looks like this:

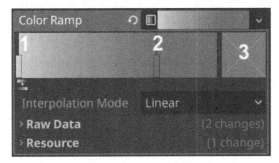

Figure 3.30: Color Ramp settings

The two rectangular sliders labeled *1* and *2* set the starting and ending colors of the gradient. Clicking on either of them will show its color in the box labeled *3*. Select slider *1* and then click box *3* to open a color picker. Choose an orange color, and then do the same for slider *2*, choosing a dark red.

Now that the particles have the correct appearance, they're lasting far too long. In the node's **Time** section, set **Lifetime** to 0.1.

Hopefully, your ship's exhaust looks somewhat like a flame. If it doesn't, feel free to adjust the properties until you are happy with how it looks.

Once the flame is looking good, it needs to be turned on and off based on the player's input. Go to `player.gd` and add `$Exhaust.emitting = false` at the beginning of `get_input()`. Then, under the `if` statement that checks for `thrust` input, add `$Exhaust.emitting = true`.

Enemy trail

You can also use particles to give the enemy saucer a sparkling trail. Add a `CPUParticles2D` to the enemy scene and configure these settings:

- **Amount**: `20`
- **Visibility/Show Behind Parent**: On
- **Emission Shape/Shape**: `Sphere`
- **Emission Shape/Sphere Radius**: `25`
- **Gravity**: `(0, 0)`

You should now have particles appearing all across the radius of the saucer (you can hide the `Sprite2D` during this part if you want to see them better). The default shape for particles is a square, but you can also use a texture for even more visual appeal. Add `res://assets/corona.png` to **Drawing/Texture**.

This image gives a nice glowing effect, but it's quite large compared to the saucer, so set **Scale/Scale Amount Max** to `0.1`. You'll also notice that this image is white on a black background. In order to look correct, it needs its **blend mode** changed. To do this, find the **Material** property and select **New CanvasItemMaterial**. There, you can change **Blend Mode** from **Mix** to **Add**.

Finally, you can make the particles fade away by using **Scale Amount Curve** in the **Scale** section, just as you did with the player particles.

Play your game and admire the effects. What else could you add with particles?

Summary

In this chapter, you learned how to work with `RigidBody2D` nodes and learned more about how Godot's physics works. You also implemented a basic finite state machine – something you'll find useful as your projects grow larger and that you'll use again in future chapters. You saw how `Container` nodes help organize and keep UI nodes aligned. Finally, you added sound effects and got your first taste of advanced visual effects by using the `Animation` and `CPUParticles2D` nodes.

You also continued to create game objects using standard Godot hierarchies, such as `CollisionShapes` attached to `CollisionObjects` and signals being used to handle communication between nodes. At this point, these practices should be starting to look familiar to you.

Are you prepared to try and remake this project on your own? Try repeating all, or even part, of this chapter without looking at the book. It's a good way to check what information you absorbed and what you need to review again. You can also try remaking it with your own variations rather than making an exact copy.

When you're ready to move on, in the next chapter, you'll make another style of game that's very popular: a platformer in the tradition of Super Mario Bros.

4

Jungle Jump – Running and Jumping in a 2D Platformer

In this chapter, you'll build a *platformer* game in the tradition of classics such as *Super Mario Bros.* Platform games are a very popular genre, and understanding how they work can help you make a variety of different game styles. If you've never attempted making one before, the player movement in platformers can be surprisingly complex to implement, and you'll see how Godot's CharacterBody2D node has features to help you in that process.

In this project, you will learn about the following:

- Using the CharacterBody2D node

- Using the Camera2D node

- Combining animations and user input to produce complex character behavior

- Designing levels using TileMap

- Creating an infinitely scrolling background using ParallaxLayer

- Transitioning between scenes

- Organizing your project and planning for expansion

Here is a screenshot of the completed game:

Figure 4.1: Completed game screenshot

Technical requirements

As with the previous projects, you'll start by downloading the art assets for the game, which can be found here: `https://github.com/PacktPublishing/Godot-Engine-Game-Development-Projects-Second-Edition/tree/main/Downloads`

You can also find the complete code for this chapter on GitHub at: `https://github.com/PacktPublishing/Godot-4-Game-Development-Projects-Second-Edition/tree/main/Chapter04%20-%20Jungle%20Jump`

Setting up the project

To create a new project, start by opening **Project Settings** so that you can configure the defaults that you'll need.

The art assets for this game use a **pixel art** style, which means they look best when the images are not smoothed, which is Godot's default setting for **texture filtering**:

Figure 4.2: Texture filtering

While it's possible to set this on each `Sprite2D`, it's more convenient to specify the default setting. Click the **Advanced** toggle in the top right and find the **Rendering/Textures** section on the left. In the settings list, scroll to the bottom and find the **Canvas Textures/Default Texture Filter** setting. Change it from **Linear** to **Nearest**.

Then, under **Display/Window**, change **Stretch/Mode** to **canvas items** and **Aspect** to **expand**. These settings will allow the user to resize the game window while preserving the image's quality. Once the project is complete, you'll be able to see the effects of this setting.

Next, you can set up the collision layers. Because this game will have several different types of collision objects that need to interact in different ways, you'll use Godot's **collision layer** system to help organize them. The layers will be more convenient to use if they're assigned names, so go to the **Layer Names | 2D Physics** section and name the first four layers like this (by typing directly in the box next to the layer number):

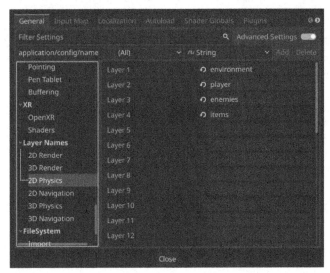

Figure 4.3: Setting physics layer names

Finally, add the following actions for the player controls to the **Input Map** area:

Action name	Key(s)
right	$D, \rightarrow$
left	$A, \leftarrow$
jump	Space
up	$S, \uparrow$
down	$W, \downarrow$

Make sure you use the exact names for the input actions since you'll be referencing them in code later.

That's all you need to set in **Project Settings**. But before you start making the player scene, you need to learn about a different type of physics node.

Introducing kinematic bodies

A platformer requires gravity, collisions, jumping, and other physics behavior, so you might think that RigidBody2D would be the perfect choice to implement the character's movement. In practice, you'll find that the more realistic physics of the rigid body are not desirable for a platform character. To the player, realism is less important than responsive control and an action feel. So, as the developer, you want to have precise control over the character's movements and collision response. For this reason, a **kinematic** style of physics is usually the better choice for a platform character.

The CharacterBody2D node is designed for implementing physics bodies that are to be controlled directly via code. These nodes detect collisions with other bodies when they move but are not affected by global physics properties such as gravity or friction. This doesn't mean that they can't be affected by gravity and other forces – just that you must calculate those forces and their effects in code; the physics engine will not move a CharacterBody2D node automatically.

When moving a CharacterBody2D node as with RigidBody2D, you should not set its position property directly. Instead, you must use the move_and_collide() or move_and_slide() methods provided by the body. These methods move the body along a given vector and instantly stop it if a collision is detected with another body. It's then up to you to decide on any **collision response**.

Collision response

After a collision, you may want the body to bounce, slide along a wall, or alter the properties of the object it hit. The way you handle collision response depends on which method you use to move the body:

move_and_collide()

When using this method, the function returns a KinematicCollision2D object upon collision. This object contains information about the collision and the colliding body. You can use this information to determine the response. Note that the function returns null when movement is completed successfully with no collision.

For example, if you want the body to bounce off the colliding object, you could use the following script:

```
extends CharacterBody2D
velocity = Vector2(250, 250)
func _physics_process(delta):
    var collision = move_and_collide(velocity * delta)
    if collision:
        velocity = velocity.bounce(collision.get_normal())
```

move_and_slide()

Sliding is a very common option for collision response. Imagine a player moving along a wall in a top-down game, or running along the ground in a platformer. While it's possible to code the response yourself after using `move_and_collide()`, `move_and_slide()` provides a convenient way to implement sliding movement. When using this method, the body will automatically slide along the surface of a colliding object. In addition, sliding collisions will allow you to detect the orientation of the surface using methods such as `is_on_floor()`.

Since this project will require you to allow the player character to run along the ground and up/down slopes, `move_and_slide()` is going to play a large role in your player's movement.

Now that you have an understanding of what kinematic bodies are, you'll use one to make the character for this game.

Creating the player scene

The Godot node that implements kinematic movement and collision is called `CharacterBody2D`.

Open a new scene and add a `CharacterBody2D` node named `Player` as the root and save the scene. Don't forget to click the **Group Selected Node(s)** button. When saving the `Player` scene, you should also create a new folder to contain it. This will help keep your project folder organized as you add more scenes and scripts.

Look at the properties of `CharacterBody2D` in the Inspector. Notice the default values of **Motion Mode** and **Up Direction**. "Grounded" mode means the body will consider one collision direction as the "floor," the opposite wall as the "ceiling," and any others as "walls" – which one is determined by **Up Direction**.

As you've done in previous projects, you'll include all the nodes the player character needs to function in the Player scene. For this game, that means handling collisions with various game objects, including platforms, enemies, and collectibles; displaying animations for actions, such as running or jumping; and attaching a camera to follow the player around the level.

Scripting the various animations can quickly become unmanageable, so you'll need to use a **finite-state machine** (**FSM**) to manage and track the player's state. See *Chapter 3* to review how a simplified FSM can be built. You'll follow a similar pattern for this project.

Collision layers and masks

A body's **Collision/Layer** property sets what layer(s) in the physics world the body is found on. `Player` needs to be assigned to the "player" layer (which you named in **Project Settings**). Similarly, **Collision/Mask** sets which layers the body can "see" or interact with. If an object is on a layer that is not in the player's **Mask**, then the player won't interact with it at all.

Set the player's **Layer** to **player** and **Mask** to **environment**, **enemies**, and **items**. Click the three dots to the right to open a list of checkboxes showing the names you've assigned to the layers:

Figure 4.4: Setting collision layers

This will ensure that the player is on the "player" layer so that other objects can be configured to detect the player or not. Setting the **Mask** value to all three layers means the player will be able to interact with objects on any of those layers.

About AnimationPlayer

Earlier in this book, you used `AnimatedSprite2D` to display the frame-based animations of your characters. This is a great tool, but it's only useful for animating the visual texture of a node. What if you want to also animate any of a node's other properties?

This is where `AnimationPlayer` comes in. This node is a very powerful tool for creating animations that can affect multiple nodes at once; you can modify any of their properties.

Animations

To set up the character's animations, follow these steps:

1. Add a `Sprite2D` node to `Player`. Drag the `res://assets/player_sheet.png` file from the **FileSystem** dock and drop it into the **Texture** property. The player animation will be saved in the form of a sprite sheet:

Figure 4.5: Sprite sheet

2. You'll use `AnimationPlayer` to handle the animations, so, in the **Animation** properties of `Sprite2D`, set **HFrames** to `19`. Then, set **Frame** to `7` to see the player standing. Finally, move `Sprite2D` upward until its feet are standing on the ground by setting **Position** to `(0, -16)`. This will make it easier to code the player's interactions later because you will know that the player's `position` property represents the location of its feet.

3. Add an `AnimationPlayer` node to the scene. You'll use this node to change the **Frame** property of `Sprite2D` to the appropriate values for each animation.

4. Before you start, review the different parts of the **Animation** panel:

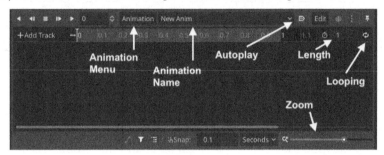

Figure 4.6: The Animation panel

5. Click the **Animation** button and select **New**. Name the new animation `idle`.

6. Set its **Length** to `0.4` seconds. Click the **Loop** icon to make the animation loop, and set the track's **Update Mode** to **Continuous**.

    Change the **Frame** property of `Sprite2D` to `7`, which is the first frame of the idle animation, and click the **keyframe** icon next to the property to add an animation track with a new keyframe:

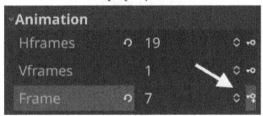

Figure 4.7: Adding a keyframe

7. Slide the play scrubber to `0.3` (you can adjust the zoom slider in the bottom right to make it easier to find). Add a keyframe for frame `10`, which is the last frame of **idle**.

8. Press the **Play** button to see the animation play. If it doesn't look correct, go back to the previous paragraph and make sure you've followed the steps exactly, especially the fact that you start on frame `7` and ended on frame `10`.

Now, repeat this process for the other animations. See the following table for a list of their settings:

Name	Length	Frames	Looping
idle	0.4	7 → 10	On
run	0.5	13 → 18	On
hurt	0.2	5 → 6	On
jump_up	0.1	11	Off
jump_down	0.1	12	Off

There are also animations in the sprite sheet for crouching and climbing, but you can add those later, once the basic movement is completed.

Collision shape

As with other bodies, `CharacterBody2D` needs a shape assigned to define its collision bounds. Add a `CollisionShape2D` node and create a new `RectangleShape2D` inside it. When sizing the shape, you want it to reach the bottom of the image (the player's feet) but be a little bit narrower than the player's image. In general, making the shape a bit smaller than the image will result in a better feel when playing, avoiding the experience of hitting something that looks like it wouldn't result in a collision.

You'll also need to offset the shape a small amount to make it fit. Setting the `CollisionShape2D` node's **Position** to (0, -10) works well. When you're done, it should look approximately like this:

Figure 4.8: Player collision shape

> **Multiple shapes**
>
> In some cases, depending on the complexity of your character and its interactions with other objects, you may want to add multiple shapes to the same object. You might have one shape at the player's feet to detect ground collisions, another on its body to detect damage, and yet another covering the player's front to detect contact with walls.

Finishing the player scene

Add a `Camera2D` node to the `Player` scene. This node will keep the game window centered on the player as it moves around the level. You can also use it to zoom in on the player since pixel art is relatively small compared to the game window's size. Remember, since you set the filtering option in **Project Settings**, the player's texture will remain pixelated and blocky when zoomed in.

To enable the camera, set the **Enabled** property to **On**, then set **Zoom** to `(2.5, 2.5)`. Values smaller than 1 zoom the camera out, while larger values zoom it in.

You'll see a pinkish-purple rectangle surrounding the player. That's the camera's **screen rectangle** and it shows what the camera will see. You can adjust the **Zoom** property to increase or decrease its size to see more or less of the world around the player.

Player states

The player character has a wide variety of behaviors, such as jumping, running, and crouching. Coding such behaviors can become very complex and hard to manage. One solution is to use Boolean variables (`is_jumping` or `is_running`, for example), but this leads to possibly confusing states (what if `is_crouching` and `is_jumping` are both `true`?) and quickly leads to _spaghetti_ code.

A better solution to this problem is to use a state machine to handle the player's current state and control the transition to other states. This concept was introduced in *Chapter 3*, and you'll expand on it in this project.

Here is a diagram of the player's states and the transitions between them:

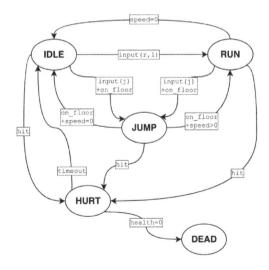

Figure 4.9: Player state diagram

As you can see, state diagrams can become quite complex, even with a relatively small number of states.

> **Other states**
>
> Note that while the sprite sheet contains animations for them, the CROUCH and CLIMB states are not included here. This is to keep the number of states manageable at the beginning of the project. Later, you'll have the opportunity to add them.

Player script

Attach a new script to the Player node. Note that the dialog shows a **Template** property with Godot's default **Basic Movement** for this node type. Uncheck the **Template** box – you won't need that example code for this project.

Add the following code to start setting up the player's state machine. As in the *Space Rocks* game, you can use an enum type to define the allowed states for the system. When you want to change the player's state, you can call change_state():

```
extends CharacterBody2D

@export var gravity = 750
@export var run_speed = 150
@export var jump_speed = -300

enum {IDLE, RUN, JUMP, HURT, DEAD}
var state = IDLE

func _ready():
    change_state(IDLE)

func change_state(new_state):
    state = new_state
    match state:
        IDLE:
            $AnimationPlayer.play("idle")
        RUN:
            $AnimationPlayer.play("run")
        HURT:
            $AnimationPlayer.play("hurt")
        JUMP:
            $AnimationPlayer.play("jump_up")
        DEAD:
            hide()
```

For now, the script only changes which animation is playing, but you'll add more state functionality later.

Player movement

The player needs three controls: left, right, and jump. Comparing the current state to which keys are pressed will trigger a state change if the transition is allowed by the state diagram's rules. Add the `get_input()` function to process the inputs and determine the result. Each `if` condition represents one of the transitions in the state diagram:

```
func get_input():
    var right = Input.is_action_pressed("right")
    var left = Input.is_action_pressed("left")
    var jump = Input.is_action_just_pressed("jump")

    # movement occurs in all states
    velocity.x = 0
    if right:
        velocity.x += run_speed
        $Sprite2D.flip_h = false
    if left:
        velocity.x -= run_speed
        $Sprite2D.flip_h = true
    # only allow jumping when on the ground
    if jump and is_on_floor():
        change_state(JUMP)
        velocity.y = jump_speed
    # IDLE transitions to RUN when moving
    if state == IDLE and velocity.x != 0:
        change_state(RUN)
    # RUN transitions to IDLE when standing still
    if state == RUN and velocity.x == 0:
        change_state(IDLE)
    # transition to JUMP when in the air
    if state in [IDLE, RUN] and !is_on_floor():
        change_state(JUMP)
```

Note that the jump check is using `is_action_just_pressed()` rather than `is_action_pressed()`. While the latter returns `true` so long as the key is held down, the former is only `true` in the frame after the key was pressed. This means that the player must press the jump key each time they want to jump.

Call this function from _physics_process(), add the pull of gravity to the player's velocity, and call the move_and_slide() method to move:

```
func _physics_process(delta):
    velocity.y += gravity * delta
    get_input()

    move_and_slide()
```

Remember, since the **Up Direction** property is set to (0, -1), any collision below the player's feet will be considered the "floor," and is_on_floor() will be set to true by move_and_slide(). You can use this fact to detect when the jump ends by adding this right after move_and_slide():

```
if state == JUMP and is_on_floor():
    change_state(IDLE)
```

The jump will look better if the animation switches from jump_up to jump_down when falling:

```
if state == JUMP and velocity.y > 0:
    $AnimationPlayer.play("jump_down")
```

Later, once the level is complete, the player will be passed a spawn location. To handle this, add this function to the script:

```
func reset(_position):
    position = _position
    show()
    change_state(IDLE)
```

With that, you have finished adding movement, and the correct animation should play for each situation. This would be a good point to stop and test the player to make sure everything is working. You can't just run the scene, though, because the player will just start falling without any surface to stand on.

Testing the movement

Create a new scene and add a Node object called Main (later, this will become your main scene). Add an instance of Player, then add a StaticBody2D node with a rectangular collision shape. Stretch the collision shape horizontally so that it's wide enough to walk back and forth on, and place it below the character:

Figure 4.10: Test scene with a platform

Since it doesn't have a `Sprite2D` node, the static body will be invisible if you run the game. In the menu, choose **Debug > Visible Collision Shapes**. This is a useful debug setting that will draw the collision shapes while the game is running. You can turn it on whenever you need to test or troubleshoot collisions.

Press **Play Scene**; you should see the player stop falling and run the `idle` animation when it hits the static body.

Before moving on, make sure that all the movements and animations are working correctly. Run and jump in all directions and check that the correct animations are playing whenever the state changes. If you find any problems, review the previous sections and make sure you didn't miss a step.

Player health

Eventually, the player is going to encounter danger, so you should add a damage system. The player will start with three hearts and lose one each time they are damaged.

Add the following to the top of the script (just after the `extends` line):

```
signal life_changed
signal died

var life = 3: set = set_life

func set_life(value):
    life = value
    life_changed.emit(life)
    if life <= 0:
        change_state(DEAD)
```

You'll emit the `life_changed` signal whenever the value of `life` changes, notifying the display to update. `dead` will be emitted when `life` reaches 0.

Add `life = 3` to the `reset()` function.

There are two possible ways for the player to be hurt: running into a spike object in the environment or being hit by an enemy. In either event, the following function can be called:

```
func hurt():
    if state != HURT:
        change_state(HURT)
```

This code is being nice to the player: if they're already hurt, they can't get hurt again (at least for a brief time until the `hurt` animation has stopped playing). Without this, it's easy to get stuck in a loop of getting hurt, resulting in a quick death.

There are a few things to do when the state changes to HURT in the change_state() function you created earlier:

```
HURT:
    $AnimationPlayer.play("hurt")
    velocity.y = -200
    velocity.x = -100 * sign(velocity.x)
    life -= 1
    await get_tree().create_timer(0.5).timeout
    change_state(IDLE)
DEAD:
    died.emit()
    hide()
```

When they're hurt, not only do they lose one life, but they are also bounced up and away from the damaging object. After a short time, the state changes back to IDLE.

Also, the input should be disabled during the HURT state. Add this to the beginning of get_input():

```
if state == HURT:
    return
```

Now, the player is ready to take damage once the rest of the game has been set up. Next, you will create the objects that the player will collect in the game.

Collectible items

Before you start making the level, you need to create some items that the player can collect, since those will be part of the level as well. The assets/sprites folder contains sprite sheets for two types of collectibles: cherries and gems.

Rather than make a separate scene for each type of item, you can use a single scene and swap out the texture property in the script. Both objects have the same behavior: animating in place and disappearing when collected by the player. You can also add a tween effect for the collection (see *Chapter 2*).

Scene setup

Start the new scene with Area2D and name it Item. Save the scene in a new items folder.

An area is a good choice for these objects because you want to detect when the player contacts them, but you don't need a collision response from them. In the Inspector, set **Collision/Layer** to collectibles (layer 4) and **Collision/Mask** to player (layer 2). This will ensure that only the Player node will be able to collect them, while the enemies will pass right through.

Add three child nodes: `Sprite2D`, `CollisionShape2D`, and `AnimationPlayer`. Drag `res://assets/sprites/cherry.png` into the `Sprite2D` node's **Texture**. Set **HFrames** to 5. Then, add a circle shape to `CollisionShape2D` and size it appropriately:

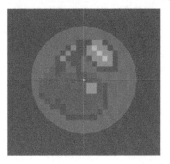

Figure 4.11: Item with collision

> **Choosing a collision size**
>
> As a general rule, you should size your collision shapes so that they benefit the player. This means that enemy hitboxes should be a little smaller than the image, while the hitboxes of beneficial items should be slightly oversized. This reduces player frustration and results in a better gameplay experience.

Add a new animation to `AnimationPlayer` (you only need one, so you can name it anything you like). Set **Length** to `1.6` seconds, **Snap** to `0.2` seconds, and **Looping** to **on**. Click the **Autoplay on Load** button so that the animation will start automatically.

Set the `Sprite2D` node's **Frame** property to `0` and click the key button to create the track. This sprite sheet only contains half the animation, so the animation needs to play the frames in the following order:

$$0 \rightarrow 1 \rightarrow 2 \rightarrow 3 \rightarrow 4 \rightarrow 3 \rightarrow 2 \rightarrow 1$$

Drag the scrubber to time `0.8` and key **Frame** at `4`. Then, key **Frame** `1` at time `1.4`. Set **Update Mode** to **Continuous** and press the **Play** button. You will have a nicely animated cherry! Note that you can also drag the `res://assets/sprites/coin.png` image into **Texture** and it will work just the same since it has the same number of frames. This will make it easy to spawn both cherries and gems in your game.

Collectible script

The `Item` script needs to do two things:

- Set the start conditions (which `texture` and `position`)
- Detect when the player overlaps

For the first part, add the following code to your new item script:

```
extends Area2D

signal picked_up

var textures = {
    "cherry": "res://assets/sprites/cherry.png",
    "gem": "res://assets/sprites/gem.png"
}

func init(type, _position):
    $Sprite2D.texture = load(textures[type])
    position = _position
```

You'll emit the `picked_up` signal when the player collects the item. In the `textures` dictionary, you will find a list of the item types and their corresponding image files. Note that you can quickly paste those paths into the script by dragging the file from **FileSystem** and dropping it into the script editor.

Next, the `init()` function sets `texture` and `position`. Your level script will use this to spawn all the items that you've placed in your level map.

Finally, connect the `body_entered` signal of `Item` and add this code:

```
func _on_item_body_entered(body):
    picked_up.emit()
    queue_free()
```

This signal will allow the game's main script to react to the item being picked up. It can add to the score, increase the player's health, or any other effect you want the item to apply.

You might have noticed that these collectible items are set up very much like the coins from *Coin Dash* were. Areas are very useful for any type of item where you need to know when it's been touched. In the next section, you'll start laying out the level scene so that you can place these collectibles.

Designing the level

For most of you, this section will take up the largest chunk of your time. Once you start designing a level, you'll find it's a lot of fun to lay out all the pieces and create challenging jumps, secret paths, and dangerous encounters.

First, you'll create a generic `Level` scene containing all the nodes and code that is common to all levels. You can then create any number of `Level` scenes that inherit from this master level.

Using TileMaps

Create a new scene and add a Node2D node named LevelBase. Save the scene in a new folder called levels. This is where you'll save all the levels you create, and they will all inherit functionality from this level_base.tscn scene. They'll all have the same node hierarchy – only the layout will be different.

A tilemap is a common tool for designing game environments using a grid of tiles. They allow you to draw a level layout by painting the tiles onto the grid rather than placing many individual nodes one at a time. They are also more efficient because they batch all the individual tile textures and collision shapes into a single game object.

Add a TileMap node; a new **TileMap** panel will appear at the bottom of the editor window. Note that it says **The edited TileMap has no TileSet resource**.

About TileSets

To draw a map using TileMap, it must have TileSet assigned. This TileSet contains all the individual tile textures, along with any collision shapes they may have.

Depending on how many tiles you may have, it can be time-consuming to create TileSet, especially for the first time. For that reason, some pre-generated tilesets have been included in the assets folder. Feel free to use those instead, but do read through the following section. It contains useful information to help you understand how TileSet works. If you'd rather use the provided tilesets, skip to the *Using the provided TileSets* section.

Creating a TileSet

In Godot, TileSet is a type of Resource. Examples of other resources include Texture, Animation, and RectangleShape2D. They are not nodes; instead, they are containers that hold a certain type of data and are usually saved as .tres files.

These are the steps for creating a TileSet container:

1. Click **New TileSet** in the **Tile Set** area of TileMap. You'll see that you now have a **TileSet** panel available, which you can select at the bottom of the editor window. You can click the two upward arrows, ⏏, to make the panel fill the editor screen. Click it again to shrink the panel.

2. The **Tiles** tab on the left-hand side of the TileSet panel is where you can place the textures that you want to slice up into tiles. Drag res://assets/environment/tileset.png into this box. A popup will appear, asking if you'd like to automatically create tiles. Select **Yes**. You'll see that boxes have been drawn around all the 16x16 pixel tiles in the image:

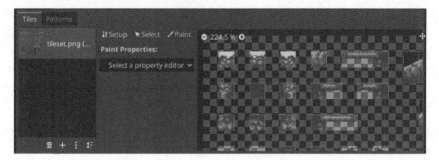

Figure 4.12: Adding a TileSet

3. Try selecting the **TileMap** panel at the bottom and then select the grass block image in the top left of the tiles. Then, click in the editor window to draw some tiles by left-clicking in the editor window. You can right-click on a tile to clear it:

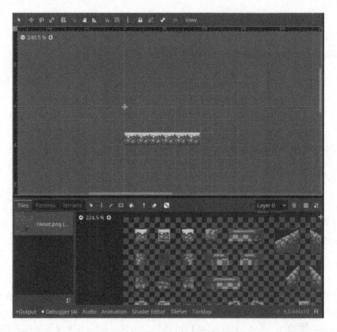

Figure 4.13: Drawing with TileMaps

If all you wanted to do was draw a background, you'd be done. However, you also need to add collisions to these tiles so that the player can stand on them.

4. Open the **TileSet** panel again and, in the Inspector, find the **PhysicsLayers** property and click **Add Element**:

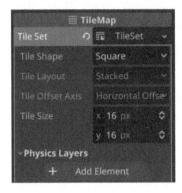

Figure 4.14: Adding a physics layer to TileSet

Since these tiles will be in the `environment` layer, you don't need to change the layer/mask settings.

5. Click **Paint** in the **TileSet** panel and, under **Paint Properties**, choose `Physics Layer 0`:

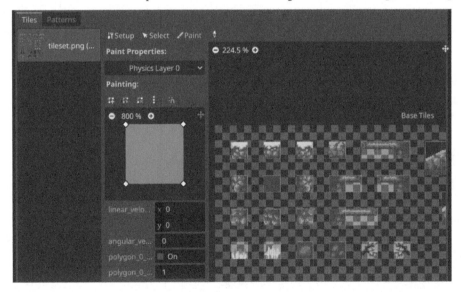

Figure 4.15: Adding collisions to tiles

6. Start clicking on the tiles to add the default square collision shape to them. If you want to edit a tile's collision shape, you can do so – click the tile again to apply the changes. If you get stuck with a shape you don't like, click the three dots and choose **Reset to default tile shape**.

You can also drag the props.png image into the texture list for some decorative items to spice up your level.

Using the provided TileSets

Pre-configured tilesets have been included in the assets download for this project. There are three to be added to three different TileMap nodes:

- World – tiles_world.tres: Ground and platform tiles
- Items – tiles_items.tres: Markers for spawning collectibles
- Danger – tiles_spikes.tres: Items that cause damage on collision

Create the Items and Danger tilemaps and add the associated tileset to the **Tile Set** property.

Add an instance of the Player scene and a Marker2D node named SpawnPoint. You can use this node to mark where in your level you want the player to start.

Attach a script to the Level node:

```
extends Node2D

func _ready():
    $Items.hide()
    $Player.reset($SpawnPoint.position)
```

Later, you'll be scanning the Items map to spawn collectibles in the designated locations. This map layer shouldn't be seen, so you could set it as hidden in the scene. However, this is easy to forget, so _ready() ensures that it's not visible during gameplay.

Designing the first level

Now, you're ready to start drawing the level! Click **Scene** > **New Inherited Scene** and choose level_base.tscn. Name the root node Level01 and save it (in the levels folder). Notice that the child nodes are colored yellow, indicating that they are **inherited** from the original level_base.tscn. If you make changes to that original scene, those changes will also appear in this scene.

Start with the World map and be creative. Do you like lots of jumps, or twisty tunnels to explore? Long runs or careful upward climbs?

Before going too far with your level design, make sure you experiment with jump distance. You can change the player's jump_speed, run_speed, and gravity properties to alter how high and how far they can jump. Set up some different gap sizes and run the scene to try them out. Don't forget to drag the SpawnPoint node to the place you want the player to start.

How you set the player's movement properties will have a big impact on how your level should be laid out. Make sure you're happy with your settings before spending too much time on the full design.

Once you have the `World` map set up, use the `Items` map to mark the locations where you'd like to spawn the cherries and gems. The tiles that mark the spawn locations are drawn with a magenta background to make them stand out. Remember, they'll be replaced at runtime and the tiles themselves won't be seen.

Once you have your level laid out, you can limit the horizontal scrolling of the player camera to match the size of the map (plus a small buffer on each end). Add this code to `level_base.gd`:

```
func _ready():
    $Items.hide()
    $Player.reset($SpawnPoint.position)
    set_camera_limits()

func set_camera_limits():
    var map_size = $World.get_used_rect()
    var cell_size = $World.tile_set.tile_size
    $Player/Camera2D.limit_left = (map_size.position.x - 5)
        * cell_size.x
    $Player/Camera2D.limit_right = (map_size.end.x + 5) *
        cell_size.x
```

The script also needs to scan the `Items` map and look for the item markers. Collecting items will add to the player's score, so you can add a variable to track that as well:

```
signal score_changed

var item_scene = load("res://items/item.tscn")

var score = 0: set = set_score

func spawn_items():
    var item_cells = $Items.get_used_cells(0)
    for cell in item_cells:
        var data = $Items.get_cell_tile_data(0, cell)
        var type = data.get_custom_data("type")
        var item = item_scene.instantiate()
        add_child(item)
        item.init(type, $Items.map_to_local(cell))
        item.picked_up.connect(self._on_item_picked_up)

func _on_item_picked_up():
    score += 1
```

```
func set_score(value):
    score = value
    score_changed.emit(score)
```

The spawn_items() function uses get_used_cells() to get a list of which cells in TileMap are not empty. These cells are in _map coordinates_, not pixel coordinates, so later, when you spawn the item, you can use map_to_local() to convert the values.

The marker tiles have a **custom data** layer attached to them (similar to the physics layer you added to the world tiles) that specifies what type they are: gem or cherry. That's then used to tell the new instance which type of item it should be.

The score variable is there to keep track of how many items the player has collected. You could have this trigger completion of the level, give a bonus, and so on.

Add spawn_items() to _ready() and try running the level. You should see gems and cherries appear wherever you've added them. Also, check that they disappear when you collect them.

Adding dangerous objects

The Danger map layer is designed to hold the spike objects that will harm the player when touched. Any tile on this TileMap will cause damage to the player! Try placing a few of them where you can easily test running into them.

In the **Node** tab, add the Danger tilemap to a group called danger so that you can easily identify it when colliding. This will also allow you to make other harmful objects upon adding them to the same group.

About slide collisions

When a CharacterBody2D node is moved with move_and_slide(), it may collide with more than one object in the same frame's movement. For example, when running into a corner, the body may hit the wall and the floor at the same time. You can use the get_slide_collision_count() function to find out how many collisions occurred; then, you can get information about each collision using get_slide_collision().

In the case of Player, you want to detect when a collision occurs against the Danger tilemap. You can do this just after using move_and_slide() in player.gd:

```
if state == HURT:
    return
for i in get_slide_collision_count():
    var collision = get_slide_collision(i)
    if collision.get_collider().is_in_group("danger"):
        hurt()
```

Note that before checking for a collision with the `danger` group, you can first check if the player is already in the HURT state. If they are, you can skip checking to see if they are colliding with a dangerous object.

The `for` loop iterates through the number of collisions given by `get_slide_collision_count()` to check each one for an object in the danger group.

Play your scene and try running into one of the spikes. You should see the player change to the HURT state (playing the animation) for a brief time before returning to IDLE. After three hits, the player will enter the DEAD state, which currently only hides the player.

Scrolling background

There are two background images in the `res://assets/environment/` folder: `back.png` and `middle.png`, for the far and near background, respectively. By placing these images behind the tilemap and scrolling them at different speeds relative to the camera, you can create an attractive illusion of depth in the background:

1. Add a `ParallaxBackground` node to the `LevelBase` scene (so that it will be present on all inherited levels). This node works with the camera to create a scrolling effect. Drag this node to the top of the scene tree so that it will be drawn behind the rest of the nodes. Next, add a `ParallaxLayer` node as its child. `ParallaxBackground` can have any number of `ParallaxLayer` children, allowing you to make multiple independently scrolling layers.

2. Add a `Sprite2D` node as a child of `ParallaxLayer` and drag the `back.png` image into its **Texture** area. Uncheck the **Offset/Centered** property so that it will be positioned relative to the screen origin. It's also a little small, so set the `Sprite2D` node's **Scale** to `(1.5, 1.5)`.

3. On `ParallaxLayer`, set **Motion/Scale** to `(0.2, 1)` (you'll need to click the **link** icon to allow the x and y values to be set separately). This setting controls how fast the background scrolls concerning the camera movement. By setting it to a number less than `1`, the image will only move a small amount as the player moves left and right.

4. You need to be sure the image repeats if your level is wider than the size of the image, so set **Motion/Mirroring** to `(576, 0)`. This is exactly the width of the image (`384` times `1.5`), so the image will be repeated when it has moved by that number of pixels.

5. Note that this background image is designed for levels that are wide rather than tall. If you jump too high, you'll see the top of the image. You can fix this by setting the top limit of the camera. If you haven't moved the background's position, its top-left corner will still be at `(0, 0)`, so you can set the **Top** limit on the camera to 0. If you have moved `ParallaxLayer` or its `Sprite2D` node, you can find the correct value to use by looking at the y value of the node's **Position**.

6. Try playing the level and running left and right. You should see the background moving by a small amount compared to how far you run.

7. Add another `ParallaxLayer` (also as a child of `ParallaxBackground`) and give it a `Sprite2D` child. This time, use the `middle.png` image. This image is much narrower than the sky image, so you'll need to adjust some settings to make it repeat properly. This is because `ParallaxBackground` needs to have images that are at least as big as the viewport area.

8. Find the `Sprite2D` node's **Texture/Repeat** property in the **CanvasItem** section and set it to `Mirror`. Then, expand the **Region** section and check the **Enabled** box. Under **Rect**, set the width and height to `(880, 368)`. `880` is the width of the image (`176`) multiplied by 5, so you will now see five repetitions of the image, each one a mirror of the last.

9. Move the `Sprite2D` node so that the image overlaps the bottom half of the ocean/sky image:

Figure 4.16: Parallax background setup

10. Set the second `ParallaxLayer` node's **Motion/Scale** to `(0.6, 1)` and **Motion/Mirroring** to `(880, 0)`. Using a higher scale factor means that this layer will scroll a little bit faster than the cloud layer behind it. Play the scene to test the effect.

Your `Level` scene's node tree should now look like this:

Figure 4.17: Level scene nodes

Your level scene now has all the pieces you need to create your level design. Do you want your player to have to make very precise jumps (a parkour level), run through a series of winding passages trying to find all the items (a maze level), or some combination of the two? This is your chance to try out some creative ideas, but make sure you leave some room for the next object you'll make: enemies.

Adding enemies

There are many different behaviors you could add for an enemy. For this game, the enemy will walk along a platform in a straight line and change direction when hitting an obstacle.

Scene setup

As before, you'll need to create a new scene to represent the enemy:

1. Start with a `CharacterBody2D` node named `Enemy` and give it three children: `Sprite2D`, `CollisionShape2D`, and `AnimationPlayer`.

2. Save the scene in a folder called `enemies`. If you decide to add more enemy types to the game, you can save them all here.

3. Set the body's collision **Layer** to **enemies** and its **Mask** to **environment**, **player**, and **enemies**. As with the player, this determines which types of objects the enemy will collide with.

4. It's also useful to group enemies together, so click the **Node** tab and add the body to a group called `enemies`.

5. Add `res://assets/sprites/opossum.png` to **Texture** and set **Animation/Hframes** to 6.

6. Add a rectangular collision shape that covers most (but not all) of the image, making sure that the bottom of the collision shape is aligned with the bottom of the opossum's feet:

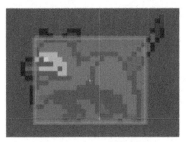

Figure 4.18: Enemy collision shape

7. Add a new animation to `AnimationPlayer` called `walk`. Set **Length** to `0.6` seconds and turn **Looping** and **Autoplay on Load** on.

8. The `walk` animation needs to have two tracks: one that sets the **Texture** property of the `Sprite2D` node and one that changes its **Frame** property. Click the key icon next to **Texture** to add the first track, then add keyframes for **Frame** 0 at time zero, and **Frame** 5 at time 0.5. Don't forget to change **Update Mode** to **Continuous**.

When finished, your animation should look like this:

Figure 4.19: Enemy animations

Scripting the enemy

By now, moving a `CharacterBody2D` node be familiar to you. Look at this script and try to understand what it's doing before reading the explanation provided after:

```
extends CharacterBody2D

@export var speed = 50
@export var gravity = 900

var facing = 1

func _physics_process(delta):
    velocity.y += gravity * delta
    velocity.x = facing * speed
    $Sprite2D.flip_h = velocity.x > 0

    move_and_slide()
    for i in get_slide_collision_count():
        var collision = get_slide_collision(i)
        if collision.get_collider().name == "Player":
            collision.get_collider().hurt()
        if collision.get_normal().x != 0:
            facing = sign(collision.get_normal().x)
            velocity.y = -100

    if position.y > 10000:
        queue_free()
```

In this script, the `facing` variable keeps track of the movement in the x direction, either `1` or `-1`. As with the player, after moving, you must check the slide collisions. If the colliding object is the player, you must call its `hurt()` function.

Next, you must check whether the colliding body's **normal** vector has an x component that isn't 0. This means it points to the left or right, which means it is a wall or other obstacle. The direction of the normal is then used to set the new facing. Giving the body a small upward velocity will give the enemy a small bounce effect when turning around, which will look more appealing.

Lastly, if for some reason the enemy falls off a platform, you don't want the game to have to track it falling forever, so you must delete any enemy whose y coordinate becomes too large.

Add an instance of Enemy to your level scene. Make sure it has some obstacles on either side and play the scene. Check that the enemy walks back and forth between the obstacles. Try putting the player in its path and verify that the player's `hurt()` function is called.

You may notice that if you jump on top of the enemy, nothing happens. We will handle that part next.

Damaging the enemy

It's not fair if the player can't hit back, so in the tradition of Mario, jumping on top of the enemy will defeat it.

Start by adding a new animation to the enemy's `AnimationPlayer` node called `death`. Set **Length** to `0.3` and **Snap** to `0.05`. Don't turn on looping for this animation.

The `death` animation will also set both **Texture** and **Frame**. Drag the `res://assets/sprites/enemy_death.png` image into the sprite's **Texture** area and then click the key to add a keyframe for it. As before, keyframe the 0 and 5 values of **Frame** at the start and end of the animation. Remember to set **Update Mode** to **Continuous**.

Add the following code to `enemy.gd` so that you have a way to trigger the death animation on the enemy:

```
func take_damage():
    $AnimationPlayer.play("death")
    $CollisionShape2D.set_deferred("disabled", true)
    set_physics_process(false)
```

When the player hits the enemy under the right conditions, it will call `take_damage()`, which plays the `death` animation, disables collision, and halts movement.

When the death animation finishes playing, it's OK to remove the enemy, so connect the `animation_finished` signal of `AnimationPlayer`:

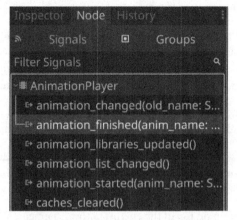

Figure 4.20: AnimationPlayer's signals

This signal is called every time any animation finishes, so you need to check if it's the correct one:

```
func _on_animation_player_animation_finished(anim_name):
    if anim_name == "death":
        queue_free()
```

To complete this process, go to the `player.gd` script and add the following code to the section of `_physics_process()` where you check the collisions. This code will check if the player hit an enemy from above:

```
for i in get_slide_collision_count():
    var collision = get_slide_collision(i)
    if collision.get_collider().is_in_group("danger"):
        hurt()
    if collision.get_collider().is_in_group("enemies"):
        if position.y < collision.get_collider().position.y:
            collision.get_collider().take_damage()
            velocity.y = -200
        else:
            hurt()
```

This code compares the y position of the player's feet to the enemy's y position to see if the player is above the enemy. If they are, the enemy should be hurt; otherwise, the player should be.

Run the level again and try jumping on the enemy to check that everything is working as expected.

Player script

You've made several additions to the player's script. Here's what the full script should look like now:

```
extends CharacterBody2D

signal life_changed
signal died

@export var gravity = 750
@export var run_speed = 150
@export var jump_speed = -300

enum {IDLE, RUN, JUMP, HURT, DEAD}
var state = IDLE
var life = 3: set = set_life

func _ready():
    change_state(IDLE)

func change_state(new_state):
    state = new_state
    match state:
        IDLE:
            $AnimationPlayer.play("idle")
        RUN:
            $AnimationPlayer.play("run")
        HURT:
            $AnimationPlayer.play("hurt")
            velocity.y = -200
            velocity.x = -100 * sign(velocity.x)
            life -= 1
            await get_tree().create_timer(0.5).timeout
            change_state(IDLE)

        JUMP:
            $AnimationPlayer.play("jump_up")
        DEAD:
            died.emit()
            hide()

func get_input():
    if state == HURT:
        return
```

```
        var right = Input.is_action_pressed("right")
        var left = Input.is_action_pressed("left")
        var jump = Input.is_action_just_pressed("jump")

        # movement occurs in all states
        velocity.x = 0
        if right:
            velocity.x += run_speed
            $Sprite2D.flip_h = false
        if left:
            velocity.x -= run_speed
            $Sprite2D.flip_h = true
    # only allow jumping when on the ground
    if jump and is_on_floor():
            change_state(JUMP)
            velocity.y = jump_speed
    # IDLE transitions to RUN when moving
    if state == IDLE and velocity.x != 0:
            change_state(RUN)
    # RUN transitions to IDLE when standing still
    if state == RUN and velocity.x == 0:
            change_state(IDLE)
    # transition to JUMP when in the air
    if state in [IDLE, RUN] and !is_on_floor():
            change_state(JUMP)

func _physics_process(delta):
    velocity.y += gravity * delta
    get_input()
    move_and_slide()
    if state == HURT:
        return
    for i in get_slide_collision_count():
        var collision = get_slide_collision(i)
        if collision.get_collider().is_in_group("danger"):
            hurt()
        if collision.get_collider().is_in_group("enemies"):
            if position.y <
            collision.get_collider().position.y:
                collision.get_collider().take_damage()
                velocity.y = -200
            else:
                hurt()
```

```
    if state == JUMP and is_on_floor():
        change_state(IDLE)
    if state == JUMP and velocity.y > 0:
        $AnimationPlayer.play("jump_down")

func reset(_position):
    position = _position
    show()
    change_state(IDLE)
    life = 3

func set_life(value):
    life = value
    life_changed.emit(life)
    if life <= 0:
        change_state(DEAD)

func hurt():
    if state != HURT:
        change_state(HURT)
```

If you're having any trouble with the player code, try to think about what part could be the problem. Is it the movement? The hit detection when running into an enemy? If you can narrow down the problem, it'll help you determine which part of the script you should be focusing on.

Make sure you're satisfied with how the player is behaving before moving on to the next section.

Game UI

As in the previous projects you've worked on, you'll need a HUD to display information during gameplay. Collecting items will increase the player's score, so that number should be displayed, as well as the player's remaining life value, which will be shown as a series of hearts.

Scene setup

Create a new scene with a MarginContainer root node named HUD and save it in a new ui folder. Set **Layout** to **Top Wide** and, in the **Theme Overrides/Constants** section of the Inspector, set the right and left margins to 50 and the top/bottom margins to 20.

Add an HBoxContainer node to keep things aligned and give it two children, Label and HBoxContainer, named Score and LifeCounter, respectively.

On the `Score` label, set the **Text** property to `100` and in the Inspector, under **Layout/Container Sizing**, check the **Expand** box. In **Label Settings**, add a new settings object to configure the font. Drag `res://assets/Kenney Thick.ttf` into the **Font** property and set **Size** to `48`. Under **Outline**, set **Size** to `16` and **Color** to black. You should see `100` displayed in white with a black outline.

For `LifeCounter`, add a `TextureRect` child and name it `L1`. Drag `res://assets/heart.png` into its **Texture** area and set **Stretch Mode** to **Keep Aspect Centered**. Select `L1` and duplicate (*Ctrl + D*) it four times so that you have a row of five hearts:

Figure 4.21: HUD node setup

When you're finished, your HUD should look like this:

Figure 4.22: HUD preview

The next step will be to add a script so that the HUD can update during the game.

Scripting the HUD

This script needs two functions that can be called to update the two values being displayed:

```
extends MarginContainer

@onready var life_counter = $HBoxContainer/LifeCounter.get_children()

func update_life(value):
    for heart in life_counter.size():
        life_counter[heart].visible = value > heart
```

```
func update_score(value):
    $HBoxContainer/Score.text = str(value)
```

Note that, in `update_life()`, you calculate how many hearts to display by setting `visible` to `false` if the number of that heart is less than the life amount.

Attaching the HUD

Open `level_base.tscn` (the base level scene, not your `Level01` scene) and add `CanvasLayer`. Add an instance of HUD as a child of this `Canvaslayer`.

Select the level's `Player` instance and connect its `life_changed` signal to the HUD's `update_life()` method:

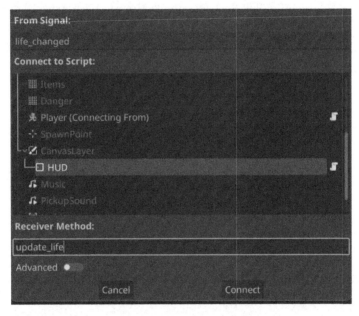

Figure 4.23: Connecting a signal

Do the same with the `score_changed` signal of the `Level` node, connecting it to the HUD's `update_score()` method.

Note that if you don't want to use the scene tree to connect the signals, or if you find the signal connection window confusing or difficult to use, you can accomplish the same thing in your script by adding these lines to the `_ready()` function of `level.gd`:

```
$Player.life_changed.connect($CanvasLayer/HUD.update_life)
score_changed.connect($CanvasLayer/HUD.update_score)
```

Play the game and verify that you can see the HUD and that it updates correctly. Make sure you collect some items and let the enemy hit you. Is your score increasing? When you're hit, do you lose one heart? Once you've checked this, you can continue to the next section and make the title screen.

Title screen

The title screen is the first thing the player will see, and the game will return to this screen when the player dies and the game ends.

Scene setup

Start with a `Control` node and set **Layout** to **Full Rect**. Add a `TextureRect` node using the `back.png` image. Set **Layout** to **Full Rect** and **Stretch Mode** to **Keep Aspect Covered**.

Add another `TextureRect`, this time using `middle.png` and setting **Stretch Mode** to **Tile**. Drag the width of the rectangle until it's wider than the screen and arrange it so that it covers the bottom half.

Add two `Label` nodes named `Title` and `Message` and set their **Text** properties to `Jungle Jump` and `Press Space to Play`, respectively. Add the font to each one as you've done before, setting the title to size `72` and the message to size `48`. Set the title's layout to **Centered** and the message's layout to **Center Bottom**.

When you're finished, the scene should look like this:

Figure 4.24: Title screen

To make the title screen more interesting, add an `AnimationPlayer` node to it. Create a new animation named `intro` and set it to autoplay. In this animation, you can animate the elements of the screen to make them move, appear, fade in, or any other effect you like.

For example, keyframe the current **Position** of `Title` at time 0.5. Then, at time 0, drag `Title` off the top of the screen and add another keyframe. Now, the title will drop onto the screen when you play the scene.

Feel free to add tracks that animate the other nodes' properties. For example, here is an animation that drops the title down, fades in the two textures, and then makes the message appear:

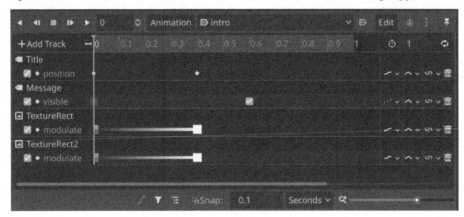

Figure 4.25: Title screen animations

This title screen has been kept simple, but you should feel free to add to it if you'd like. You could show an example of some platforms, add an animation of the character running across the screen, or some other game art. But what happens when the player hits "start"? For this, you need to load the first level in the main scene.

Setting up the main scene

You've made some level scenes, but eventually, you're going to want to make more than one. How does the game know which one to load? Your `Main` scene is going to take care of that.

Delete any extra nodes you added to `main.tscn` when you were testing the player's movement. This scene will now be responsible for loading the current level. Before it can do that, however, you need a way to keep track of the current level. You can't keep track of that variable in the level scene because that will be replaced with a newly loaded level when it ends. To keep track of data that needs to be carried from scene to scene, you can use an **autoload**.

About autoloads

In Godot, you can configure a script or scene as an autoload. This means that the engine will automatically load it at all times. Even if you change the current scene in `SceneTree`, the autoloaded node will remain. You can also refer to that autoloaded scene by name from any other node in your game.

In the **Script** editor, create a new script named `game_state.gd` and add the following code:

```
extends Node

var num_levels = 2
var current_level = 0

var game_scene = "res://main.tscn"
var title_screen = "res://ui/title.tscn"

func restart():
    current_level = 0
    get_tree().change_scene_to_file(title_screen)

func next_level():
    current_level += 1
    if current_level <= num_levels:
        get_tree().change_scene_to_file(game_scene)
```

You should set `num_levels` to the number of levels you've created in the `levels` folder. Make sure you name them consistently as `level_01.tscn`, `level_02.tscn`, and so on so that they can be found easily.

To add this script as an autoload, open **Project Settings** and find the **Autoload** tab. Click the folder icon to choose `game_state.gd` and then click the **Add** button.

Next, add this script to your `Main` scene:

```
extends Node

func _ready():
    var level_num = str(GameState.current_level).pad_zeros(2)
    var path = "res://levels/level_%s.tscn" % level_num
    var level = load(path).instantiate()
    add_child(level)
```

Now, whenever the `Main` scene is loaded, it will include the level scene that corresponds to the current level.

The title screen needs to transition to the game scene, so attach this script to the `Title` node:

```
extends Control

func _input(event):
    if event.is_action_pressed("ui_select"):
```

```
GameState.next_level()
```

Finally, you can call the `restart()` function when the player dies by adding it to `level.gd`. In the `Level` scene, connect the `Player` instance's `died` signal:

```
func _on_player_died():
    GameState.restart()
```

You should now be able to play through the game fully. Make sure `title.tscn` is set as the game's main scene (that is, the one that runs first). If you've previously set a different scene to be the "main" scene, you can change this in **Projects Settings** under **Application/Run**:

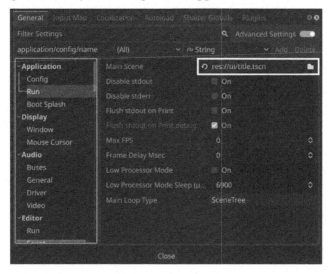

Figure 4.26: Choosing a main scene

Transitioning between levels

Your levels now need a way to transition from one to the next. In the `res://assets/environment/props.png` sprite sheet, there is an image of a door that you can use for your level's exit. Finding and walking into the door will take the player to the next level.

Door scene

Make a new scene with an `Area2D` node named `Door` and save it in the `items` folder. Add a `Sprite2D` node and use the `props.png` image as **Texture**. Under **Region**, click **Enabled**, and then click the **Edit Region** button to select the door image from the sprite sheet. Then, in **Offset/Offset**, set **y** to `-8`. This will ensure that when the door is placed at the tile location, it will be positioned correctly.

Add a `CollisionShape2D` node and give it a rectangular shape that covers the door. Put the door on the `items` layer and set its mask so that it only scans the `player` layer.

This scene doesn't need a script because you're just going to use its `body_entered` signal in the level script.

To place the door in the level, you can use the door object from the `tiles_items` tileset, which you are using in your `Items` tilemap to place the cherries and gems. Place a door in your level and open `level.gd`.

At the top of `level.gd`, define the door scene:

```
var door_scene = load("res://items/door.tscn")
```

Then, update `spawn_items()` so that it also instantiates doors:

```
func spawn_items():
    var item_cells = $Items.get_used_cells(0)
    for cell in item_cells:
        var data = $Items.get_cell_tile_data(0, cell)
        var type = data.get_custom_data("type")
        if type == "door":
            var door = door_scene.instantiate()
            add_child(door)
            door.position = $Items.map_to_local(cell)
            door.body_entered.connect(_on_door_entered)
        else:
            var item = item_scene.instantiate()
            add_child(item)
            item.init(type, $Items.map_to_local(cell))
            item.picked_up.connect(self._on_item_picked_up)
```

Add the function that will be called when the player touches the door:

```
func _on_door_entered(body):
    GameState.next_level()
```

Play the game and try walking into the door. If you've set `num_levels` in `game_state.gd` to a number greater than 1, the game will attempt to load `level_02.tscn` when you touch the door.

Screen settings

Recall that at the beginning of this chapter, you set **Stretch/Mode** and **Aspect** in **Project Settings** to `canvas_items` and expand, respectively. Run the game, and then try resizing the game window. Notice that if you make the window wider, you can see more of the game world to the player's left/right. This is what the expand value is doing.

If you want to prevent this, you can set it to keep instead, which will always show the same amount of the game world as shown by the camera. However, it also means that if you make your window a different shape than the game, you'll get black bars to fill in the extra space.

Alternatively, setting ignore will not display the black bars, but the game content will be stretched to fill the space, distorting the image.

Take some time to experiment with the various settings and decide which one you prefer.

Finishing touches

Now that you've completed the main structure of the game, and hopefully designed a few levels for the player to enjoy, you can consider making some additions to improve the gameplay. In this section, you'll find a few more suggested features – add them as-is or adjust them to your liking.

Sound effects

As with the previous projects, you can add audio effects and music to improve the experience. In res://assets/audio/, you'll find audio files you can use for different game events, such as player jump, enemy hit, and item pickup. There are also two music files: Intro Theme for the title screen and Grasslands Theme for the level scene.

Adding these to the game will be left to you, but here are a few tips:

- You may find it helpful to adjust the volume of individual sounds. This can be set with the **Volume dB** property. Setting a negative value will reduce the sound's volume.

- You can attach the music to the master level.tscn scene; that music will be used for all levels. You could also attach separate music to individual levels if you want to set a certain mood.

- Your first thought might be to put AudioStreamPlayer on the Item scene to play the pickup sound. However, since the pickup is deleted when the player touches it, that won't work well. Instead, put the audio player in the Level scene, since that's where the result of the pickup is handled (increasing the score).

Double jumping

Double jumps are a popular platforming feature. The player gets a second, usually smaller, upwards boost if they press the jump key a second time while in the air. To implement this feature, you need to add a few things to the player script.

First, you will need variables to track the number of jumps and determine how big the second boost will be:

```
@export var max_jumps = 2
@export var double_jump_factor = 1.5
```

```
var jump_count = 0
```

When entering the JUMP state, reset the number of jumps:

```
JUMP:
    $AnimationPlayer.play("jump_up")
    jump_count = 1
```

In get_input(), allow the jump if it meets the conditions that have been. Put this before the if statement where you check if the player is on the floor:

```
if jump and state == JUMP and jump_count < max_jumps and jump_count >
0:
    $JumpSound.play()
    $AnimationPlayer.play("jump_up")
    velocity.y = jump_speed / double_jump_factor
    jump_count += 1
```

In _physics_process(), when you land on the ground, reset the jump count:

```
if state == JUMP and is_on_floor():
    change_state(IDLE)
    jump_count = 0
```

Play your game and try out the double jumps. Note that this code makes the second jump 2/3rds the size of the upward speed of the initial jump. You can adjust this according to your preferences.

Dust particles

Spawning dust particles at the character's feet is a low-effort effect that can add a lot of character to your player's movements. In this section, you'll add a small puff of dust to the player's feet that is emitted whenever they land on the ground. This adds a sense of weight and impact to the player's jumps.

Add a CPUParticles2D node to the Player scene and name it Dust. Set the following properties:

Property	Value
Amount	20
Lifetime	0.45
One Shot	On
Speed Scale	2
Explosiveness	0.7

Emission Shape	`Rectangle`
Rect Extents	`1, 6`
Initial Velocity Max	`10`
Scale Amount Max	`3`
Position	`-2, 0`
Rotation	`-90`

The default particle color is white, but the dust effect will look better in a tan shade. It should also fade away so that it appears to dissipate. This can be accomplished with `Gradient`. In the **Color/Color Ramp** area, select **New Gradient**.

`Gradient` has two colors: a start color on the left and an end color on the right. These can be selected using the small rectangles at either end of the gradient. Clicking on the large square on the right allows you to set the color for the selected rectangle:

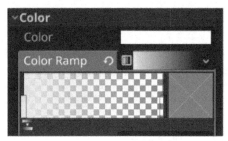

Figure 4.27: Color Ramp

Set the start color to a tan shade, and set the end to the same color, but with the alpha value set to 0. You should see a continuously puffing smoke effect. In the Inspector, set **One Shot** to on. Now, the particles will only emit once, each time you check the **Emitting** box.

Feel free to alter the properties that have been provided here. Experimenting with particle effects can be great fun, and often, you'll stumble upon a very nice effect just by tinkering.

Once you're happy with its appearance, add the following to the player's `_physics_process()` code:

```
if state == JUMP and is_on_floor():
    change_state(IDLE)
    $Dust.emitting = true
```

Run the game and observe the puff of dust every time your character lands on the ground.

Ladders

The player sprite sheet includes frames for a climbing animation, and the tileset contains ladder images. Currently, the ladder tiles do nothing – in `TileSet`, they do not have any collision shape assigned. That's OK because you don't want the player to collide with the ladders – you want them to be able to move up and down on them.

Player code

Start by selecting the player's `AnimationPlayer` node and adding a new animation called `climb`. Its **Length** should be `0.4` and it should be set to **loop**. The **Frame** values for `Sprite2D` are *0 -> 1 -> 0 -> 2.*

Go to `player.gd` and add a new state, `CLIMB`, to the `state` enum. In addition, add two new variable declarations at the top of the script:

```
@export var climb_speed = 50

var is_on_ladder = false
```

You'll use `is_on_ladder` to keep track of whether the player is on a ladder or not. Using this, you can decide whether the up and down actions should have any effect.

In `change_state()`, add a condition for the new state:

```
CLIMB:
    $AnimationPlayer.play("climb")
```

In `get_input()`, you need to check for the input actions and then determine if they change the state:

```
var up = Input.is_action_pressed("climb")
var down = Input.is_action_pressed("crouch")

if up and state != CLIMB and is_on_ladder:
    change_state(CLIMB)
if state == CLIMB:
    if up:
        velocity.y = -climb_speed
        $AnimationPlayer.play("climb")
    elif down:
        velocity.y = climb_speed
        $AnimationPlayer.play("climb")
    else:
        velocity.y = 0
        $AnimationPlayer.stop()
if state == CLIMB and not is_on_ladder:
    change_state(IDLE)
```

Here, you have three new conditions to check. First, if the player is not in the CLIMB state but is on a ladder, then pressing up should make the player start climbing. Second, if the player is currently climbing, then the up and down inputs should make them move up and down the ladder, but stop the animation from playing if no action is pressed. Finally, if the player leaves the ladder while climbing, they leave the CLIMB state.

You also need to make sure that gravity doesn't pull the player downward while they're on a ladder. Add a condition to the gravity code in _physics_process():

```
if state != CLIMB:
    velocity.y += gravity * delta
```

Now, the player is ready to climb, which means you can add some ladders to your level.

Level setup

Add an Area2D node named Ladders to the Level scene, but don't add a collision shape to it yet. Connect its body_entered and body_exited signals and set its collision **Layer** to items and **Mask** to player. This ensures that only the player can interact with the ladder. These signals are how you'll let the player know they are or aren't on a ladder:

```
func _on_ladders_body_entered(body):
    body.is_on_ladder = true

func _on_ladders_body_exited(body):
    body.is_on_ladder = false
```

Now, the level needs to look for any ladder tiles and add collision shapes to the Ladders area whenever it finds one. Add the following function to level.gd and call it in _ready():

```
func create_ladders():
    var cells = $World.get_used_cells(0)
    for cell in cells:
        var data = $World.get_cell_tile_data(0, cell)
        if data.get_custom_data("special") == "ladder":
            var c = CollisionShape2D.new()
            $Ladders.add_child(c)
            c.position = $World.map_to_local(cell)
            var s = RectangleShape2D.new()
            s.size = Vector2(8, 16)
            c.shape = s
```

Note that the collision shapes you're adding are only 8 pixels wide. If you make the shape the full width of the ladder tile, then the player will still look as though they're climbing even when they're hanging off the side, which looks a bit odd.

Try it out – go to one of your level scenes and place some ladder tiles anywhere you'd like on your `World` tile map. Play the scene and try climbing the ladders.

Note that if you're at the top of a ladder and step on it, you'll fall to the bottom rather than climb down (although pressing up as you fall will cause you to grab the ladder). If you prefer to automatically transition to the climbing state, you can add an additional falling check in `_physics_process()`.

Moving platforms

Moving platforms are a fun addition to your level design toolkit. In this section, you'll make a moving platform that you can place anywhere on your level and set its movement and speed.

Start with a new scene using a `Node2D` node and name it `MovingPlatform`. Save the scene and add `TileMap` as a child. Since your platform art is all in sprite sheets and they've already been sliced into tiles and had collisions added, this will make your platform easy to draw. Add `tiles_world.tres` as **Tile Set**. You'll also need to check the **Collision Animatable** box, which will make sure the collisions work properly even while moving.

Draw a few tiles into `TileMap`, but make sure to start at the origin, `(0, 0)`, so that things will line up cleanly. These tiles work well for a floating platform:

Figure 4.28: Floating platform

Add a script to the root node and start with these variables:

```
@export var offset = Vector2(320, 0)
@export var duration = 10.0
```

These will allow you to set the movement amount and speed. `offset` is relative to the starting point, and since it's a `Vector2` node, you can have platforms that move horizontally, vertically, or diagonally. `duration` is measured in seconds and represents how long the *complete* cycle will take.

The platform will always be moving, so you can start the animation in `_ready()`. It will use a `tween` method to animate the position in two steps: from the start position to the offset position and vice versa:

```
func _ready():
    var tween = create_tween().set_process_mode(
        Tween.TWEEN_PROCESS_PHYSICS)
```

```
tween.set_loops().set_parallel(false)
tween.tween_property($TileMap, "position", offset,
    duration / 2.0).from_current()
tween.tween_property($TileMap, "position",
    Vector2.ZERO, duration / 2.0)
```

Here are a few notes about tween usage:

- You need to set the process mode so that the movement will be synced to physics and the player will be able to collide properly with the platform (that is, stand on it).

- `set_loops()` tells `tween` to repeat once finished.

- `set_parallel(false)` tells `tween` to perform the two property tweens sequentially rather than at the same time.

- You can also experiment with other tween curves. Adding `tween.set_trans(Tween. TRANS_SINE)`, for example, will make the platform slow down at the ends of the movement for a more natural look. Try experimenting with the other transition types.

Now, you can add instances of `MovingPlatform` to the level scene. To make sure things line up properly, make sure you turn on grid snapping:

Figure 4.29: Enabling grid snapping

The default value is (8, 8), but you can change it by clicking the three dots next to the icon and choosing **Configure Snap**.

When you run the game now, you will have a lot more to interact with. The ladders and moving platforms give you a lot more possibilities for your level designs. But you don't have to stop there! Considering everything you've done in this chapter, there are many other features that you could still add. The player animation includes a "crouching" animation – what if the enemies could throw things at the player that could be ducked under? Many platformer games include additional movement mechanics such as sliding down slopes, wall jumps, changing gravity, and many more. Choose one and see if you can add it.

Summary

In this chapter, you learned how to use the `CharacterBody2D` node to create arcade-style physics for player movement. This is a powerful node that can be used for a wide variety of game objects – not just platform characters.

You learned about the `TileMap` node for level design – a powerful tool with even more features than you used in this project. An entire chapter could be written on all of the different things you can do with it. For more information, see the *Using TileMaps* page on the Godot documentation website: `https://docs.godotengine.org/en/latest/tutorials/2d/using_tilemaps.html`.

`Camera2D` and `ParallaxBackground` are also key tools for any game where you want to move around in a world that's bigger than the size of the screen. The camera node in particular will be a node that you'll use in most 2D projects.

You also made extensive use of what you learned in earlier projects to tie everything together. Hopefully, at this point, you have a good grasp of the scene system and how a Godot project is structured.

Once again, before moving on, take a few moments to play your game and look through its various scenes and scripts to review how you built it. Review any sections of this chapter that you found particularly tricky. And most importantly, before moving on, try to make some changes to the project.

In the next chapter, you'll make the jump to 3D!

5

3D Minigolf: Dive into 3D by Building a Minigolf Course

The previous projects in this book have been designed in 2D space. This is intentional to introduce the features and concepts of Godot while keeping the projects' scopes limited. In this chapter, you'll venture into the 3D side of game development. For some, 3D development feels significantly more difficult to manage. For others, it is more straightforward. In either case, there is certainly an additional layer of complexity for you to understand.

If you've never worked with any kind of 3D software before, you may find yourself encountering many new concepts. This chapter will explain them as much as possible, but remember to refer to the Godot documentation whenever you need a more in-depth understanding of a particular topic.

The game you'll make in this chapter is called *3D Minigolf*. In it, you'll build a small minigolf course, a ball, and an interface for aiming and shooting the ball toward the hole.

Here are some of the things you'll learn in this chapter:

- Navigating Godot's 3D editor
- Node3D and its properties
- Importing 3D meshes and using 3D collision shapes
- How to use 3D cameras
- Setting up lighting and environment
- An introduction to PBR and materials

Before diving in, a brief introduction to 3D in Godot.

Technical requirements

Download the game assets from the following link and unzip them into your new project folder:

`https://github.com/PacktPublishing/Godot-4-Game-Development-Projects-Second-Edition/tree/main/Downloads`

You can also find the complete code for this chapter on GitHub at: `https://github.com/PacktPublishing/Godot-4-Game-Development-Projects-Second-Edition/tree/main/Chapter05%20-%203D%20Minigolf`

Introduction to 3D

One of the strengths of Godot is its ability to handle both 2D and 3D games. Much of what you've learned earlier in this book will apply equally well in 3D – nodes, scenes, signals, etc. But changing from 2D to 3D also brings with it a whole new layer of complexity and capabilities. First, you'll find that there are some additional features available in the 3D editor window, and it's a good idea to familiarize yourself with how to navigate.

Orienting in 3D space

Open a new project and click on the **3D** button at the top of the editor window to see the 3D project view:

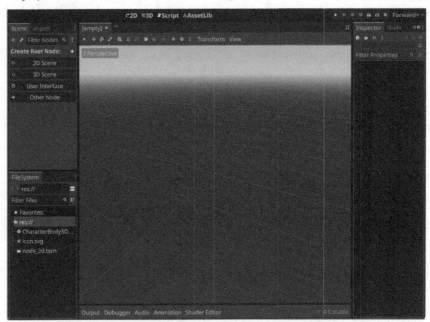

Figure 5.1: The 3D workspace

The first things you should notice are the three colored lines in the center. These are the x (red), y (green), and z (blue) axes. The point where they meet is the **origin**, with coordinates of (0, 0, 0).

> **3D coordinates**
>
> Just as you used Vector2(x, y) to indicate a position in 2D space, you'll use Vector3(x, y, z) to describe a position in three dimensions.

One issue that often arises when working in 3D is that different applications use different conventions for orientation. Godot uses the **Y-UP** orientation, so when looking at the axes, if x is pointing to the left/right, then y is up/down and z is forward/back. If you use other popular 3D software, you may find that some of them use **Z-Up**. It's good to be aware of this, as it can lead to confusion when moving between different programs.

Another important thing to be aware of is the unit of measure. In 2D, Godot measures everything in pixels, which makes sense as the natural basis for measurement when drawing on the screen. However, when working in 3D space, pixels aren't really useful. Two objects of the same size will occupy different areas on the screen depending on how far away they are from the camera (more about cameras soon). For this reason, in 3D space, all objects in Godot are measured in generic units. While it's most common to refer to them as "meters," you're free to call these units whatever you like: inches, millimeters, or even light years, depending on the scale of your game world.

Godot's 3D editor

Before moving too deeply into building a game, it will be useful to review how to navigate in 3D space. The view camera is controlled using the mouse and keyboard:

- *Mouse wheel up/down*: Zoom in/out on the current target
- *Middle button + drag*: Orbit the camera around the current target
- *Shift + middle button + drag*: Pan the camera up/down/left/right
- *Right button + drag*: Rotate the camera in place

Note that some of these movements are based on a camera target, or **focus**. To focus on an object in space, you can select it and press *F*.

> **Freelook navigation**
>
> If you're familiar with popular 3D games such as *Minecraft*, you can press *Shift + F* to switch to FreeLook mode. In this mode, you can use the *W/A/S/D* keys to fly around the scene while aiming with the mouse. Press *Shift + F* again to exit FreeLook mode.

You can also affect the camera's view by clicking on the **Perspective** label in the upper-left corner of the viewport. Here, you can snap the camera to a particular orientation such as **Top View** or **Front View**:

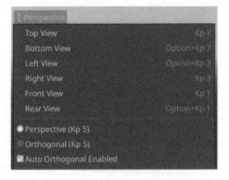

Figure 5.2: Perspective menu

This can be especially useful on large displays when combined with the use of multiple viewports. Click the **View** menu and you can split the screen into multiple views, allowing you to see an object from all sides simultaneously.

Keyboard shortcuts

Note that each of these menu options has a keyboard shortcut associated with it. You can click on **Editor** -> **Editor Settings** -> **3D** to see and adjust the keyboard shortcuts to your liking.

Adding 3D objects

It's time to add your first 3D node. Just as all 2D nodes inherit from Node2D, which provides properties such as **Position** and **Rotation**, 3D nodes inherit from Node3D, which provides spatial properties. Add one to the scene and you'll see the following:

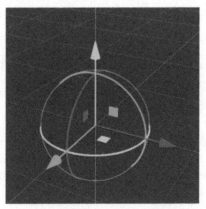

Figure 5.3: Node3D with a gizmo

That colorful object you see is not the node, but rather a 3D **gizmo**. The gizmo is a tool that allows you to move and rotate objects in space. The three rings control rotation, while the three arrows move the object along the three axes. Notice that the rings and arrows are color-coded to match the axis colors. The arrows move the object *along* the corresponding axis, while the rings rotate the object *around* a particular axis. There are also three small squares that lock one axis and allow you to move along the object in a plane.

Take a few minutes to experiment and get familiar with the gizmo. Delete the node and add another if you find yourself getting lost.

Sometimes the gizmo gets in the way. You can click on the mode icons to restrict yourself to only one type of transformation: **Movement**, **Rotation**, or **Scaling**:

Figure 5.4: Select mode icons

The *Q*/*W*/*E*/*R* keys are shortcuts for these buttons, allowing you to quickly change between modes.

Global versus local space

By default, the gizmo control operates in a global space. Try rotating the object – no matter how you turn it, the gizmo's movement arrows still point along the global axes. Now try this: put the Node3D node back into its original position and orientation (or delete it and add a new one). Rotate the object around one axis and then click the **Use Local Space** button (note the **T** shortcut):

Figure 5.5: Toggling Local Space mode

Observe what happens to the gizmo arrows. They now point along the object's *local* axes and not the world's axes. When you click and drag the arrows, they move the object relative to its own rotation. You can toggle back to global space by clicking the button again. Switching back and forth between these two modes can make it much easier to place an object exactly where you want it.

Transforms

Look at the Inspector for Node3D. Under the **Transform** section, you'll see the node's **Position**, **Rotation**, and **Scale** properties. As you move the object around, you'll see these values change. Just as in 2D, these values are *relative* to the node's parent.

Together, these three quantities make up the node's **transform** property. When changing the node's spatial properties in code, you have access to its `transform` property, which is a Godot `Transform3D` object. `Transform3D` has two sub-properties: `origin` and `basis`. The `origin` property represents the body's position, while the `basis` property contains three vectors that define the body's local coordinate axes. Think of the three axis arrows in the gizmo when you were in **Local Space** mode.

You'll see how to use these properties later in this section.

Meshes

Just like `Node2D`, a `Node3D` node has no size or appearance of its own. In 2D, you added `Sprite2D` to display a texture attached to a node. In 3D, you'll typically want to add a **mesh**. A mesh is a mathematical description of a three-dimensional shape. It consists of a collection of points called **vertices**. These vertices are connected by lines, called **edges**, and multiple edges (at least three) together make a **face**.

A cube, for example, is composed of eight vertices, twelve edges, and six faces:

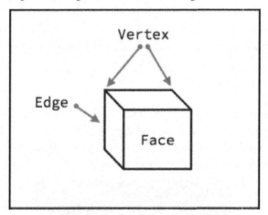

Figure 5.6: Vertices, edges, and faces

If you've ever used 3D design software, this may already be familiar to you. If you haven't, and you're interested in learning about 3D modeling, *Blender* is a very popular open source tool for designing 3D objects. You can find many tutorials and lessons on the internet to help you get started with Blender.

Primitives

If you haven't already created or downloaded a 3D model, or if you just need a simple shape quickly, Godot has the ability to create certain 3D meshes directly. Add a `MeshInstance3D` node as a child of your `Node3D` node, and in the Inspector, look for the **Mesh** property:

Figure 5.7: Adding a new mesh

These predefined shapes are called **primitives**, and they represent a handy collection of common useful shapes. Select **New BoxMesh** and you'll see a cube appear on the screen.

Importing meshes

Whatever modeling software you may use, you will need to export your models in a format that is readable by Godot. Godot supports a number of file formats for importing:

- glTF – supported in both text (.gltf) and binary (.glb) versions
- DAE (COLLADA) – an old format that is still supported
- OBJ (Wavefront) – supported, but limited due to the format limitations
- ESCN – a Godot-specific file format that Blender can export
- FBX – a commercial format that has limited support

The recommended format is .gltf. It has the most features and is very well supported in Godot. See the appendix for details about exporting .gltf files from Blender for use in Godot.

You'll see how to import some pre-built .gltf scenes later in this chapter.

Cameras

Try running the scene with your cube mesh. Where is it? In 3D, you won't see anything in the game viewport unless you have a `Camera3D` camera in the scene. Add one, and you'll see a new node that looks like this:

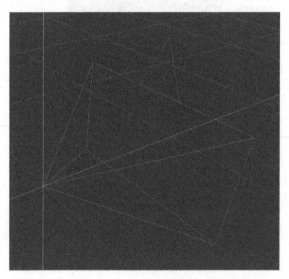

Figure 5.8: Camera widget

Use the camera's gizmo to position it a little bit above and point toward the cube:

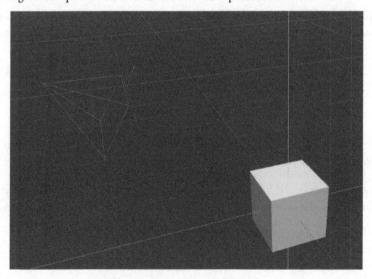

Figure 5.9: Aiming the camera

The pinkish-purple, pyramid-shaped object is called the camera's **frustum**. It represents the camera's view and can be made narrow or wide to affect the camera's **field of view**. The triangular shape at the top of the frustum indicates the camera's "up" direction.

As you're moving the camera around, you can press the **Preview** button in the upper-right of the viewport to check what the camera sees. Go ahead and experiment with positioning the camera and adjusting its **FOV**.

Orientation

Note that the camera's frustum faces along the -**Z** axis. This is the forward direction in Godot's 3D space. For example, this is what you would do if you wanted to move a 3D object along its local forward axis where `transform.basis` is the object's local set of axes:

```
position += -transform.basis.z * speed * delta
```

These new concepts and editor functions will help you to navigate and work in 3D space. Refer back to this section if you need a reminder of what a particular 3D-related term means. In the next section, you'll start setting up your first 3D project.

Project setup

Now that you've learned how to navigate in Godot's 3D editor, you're ready to start on the minigolf game. As with the other projects, download the game assets from the following link and unzip them into your project folder. The unzipped `assets` folder contains images, 3D models, and other items you'll need to complete the game.

Create a new project and download the project assets from `https://github.com/ PacktPublishing/Godot-Engine-Game-Development-Projects-Second-Edition`.

You'll notice a few different folders in `assets`. The `courses` folder has some pre-built minigolf holes for you to try out and compare to the ones you make. Don't look at them yet – try and follow the steps to make your own first.

This game will use the left mouse click as an input. Open **Project Settings** and select the **Input Map** tab. Add a new action called `click` and then click the plus sign to add the **Left Mouse Button** input to it:

Figure 5.10: Assigning a mouse button input

While you're in **Project Settings**, you can also set how the game behaves when the game window is resized. During gameplay, the user may choose to resize the window, which could disrupt the layout of your UI or show a distorted view of the game. To prevent this, navigate to the **Display/Window** section and find the **Stretch/Mode** setting. Change it to **viewport**:

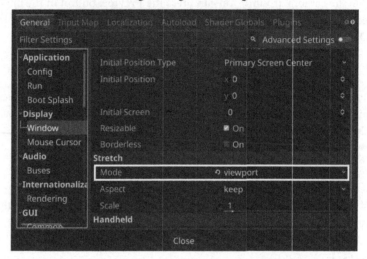

Figure 5.11: Setting window stretch mode

That completes the setup of the project. Now, you can move on to building the first part of the game: the minigolf course.

Creating the course

For the first scene, add a `Node3D` node called `Hole` and save the scene. As you did in *Jungle Jump*, you're going to make a generic scene containing all the nodes and code that any hole will need, then inherit from this scene to make as many individual holes as you want to have in the game.

Next, add a `GridMap` node to the scene.

Understanding GridMaps

`GridMap` is the 3D equivalent of the `TileMap` node you used earlier in the book. It allows you to use a collection of meshes (contained in a `MeshLibrary` collection – similar to `TileSet`) and lay them out in a grid. Because it operates in 3D, you can stack the meshes in any direction, although for this project you'll stick to one plane.

Making a MeshLibrary collection

In the `res://assets/` folder, you'll find a pre-generated `MeshLibrary` feature named `golf_tiles.tres` containing all the necessary course parts along with their collision shapes.

To create your own `MeshLibrary` function, you'll make a 3D scene containing the individual meshes you want to use, add collisions to them, and then export that scene into a `MeshLibrary` collection. If you open `golf_tiles.tscn`, you'll see the original scene that was used to create `golf_tiles.tres`.

In this scene, you'll see all the individual golf course tile meshes, as they were imported from Blender, where they were originally modeled. To add collision shapes to each one, Godot has a handy shortcut: select a mesh and you'll see a **Mesh** menu appear in the toolbar at the top of the viewport:

Figure 5.12: The Mesh menu

Select **Create Trimesh Static Body** and Godot will add a `StaticBody3D` node along with a `CollisionShape3D` node using the mesh's data.

Once all the collisions are added, you can choose **Scene -> Export As -> Mesh Library** to convert the scene into a Resource that `GridMap` can use.

Drawing the first hole

Drag the `MeshLibrary` file into the **Mesh Library** property of the `GridMap` node. You'll see a list of the available tiles appear on the right side of the editor viewport.

To match the size of the tiles, set **Cell/Size** to `(1, 1, 1)`.

To make sure the collisions with the ball will look good, find **Physics Material** and set its **Rough** setting to **On** and **Bounce** to `0.5`:

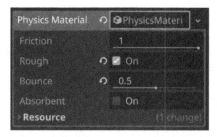

Figure 5.13: Working with Physics Material

Try drawing by selecting a tile piece from the list and placing it in the scene by left-clicking. You can rotate a piece around the y axis by pressing **S**. To remove a tile, right-click on it.

For now, stick to a simple layout. You can get fancy later when everything is working:

Figure 5.14: Example course layout

You can check out what this will look like when the game runs. Add a `Camera3D` feature to the scene and move it to a position where it can look down on the course. Remember, you can press **Preview** to check what the camera sees.

Play the scene. You'll notice that everything is very dark, unlike how it looks in the editor window. By default, a 3D scene has no *environment* or *lighting* configured.

Environment and lighting

Lighting is a complex subject all on its own. Choosing where to place lights and how they're configured can dramatically affect how a scene looks.

Godot provides three lighting nodes in 3D:

- `OmniLight3D`: For light that is emitted in all directions, such as from a light bulb
- `DirectionalLight3D`: Light from a distant source, such as sunlight
- `SpotLight3D`: A cone-shaped light projected from a point, similar to a flashlight or lantern

In addition to placing individual lights, you can also set up *ambient* light – light that is produced by the environment – using a `WorldEnvironment` node.

Rather than start from scratch, Godot will let you start with the default lighting setup that you see in the editor window using the buttons in the toolbar:

Figure 5.15: Lighting and environment settings

The first two buttons allow you to toggle the preview sun (directional light) and environment. Note that the environment doesn't just affect lighting, it generates a sky texture as well.

If you click on the three dots, you can see the default settings for these. Click the **Add** buttons to add them both as nodes in your scene. You'll now have the WorldEnvironment node and a DirectionalLight3D node in your scene.

If you zoom in on your mesh, you may notice that the shadows don't look very good. The default shadow settings need to be adjusted, so select DirectionalLight3D and change **Max Distance** from 100 to 40.

Adding the hole

Now that you have the course laid out, you need a way to detect when the ball falls into the hole.

Add an `Area3D` node named `Hole`. This node works exactly like its 2D version – it can signal when a body enters its defined shape. Add a `CollisionShape3D` child to the area. In the **Shape** property, choose **New CylinderShape3D** and set its **Height** to 0.25 and **Radius** to 0.08.

Position `Hole` where you placed the hole tile for your course. Make sure the cylinder shape doesn't project above the top of the hole, or the ball will count as "in" when it hasn't dropped in yet. You might find it useful to use the **Perspective** button and change to **Top View** to make sure you've got it centered properly:

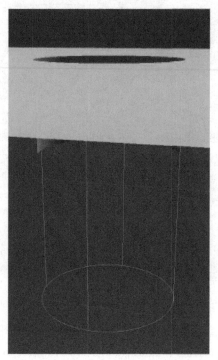

Figure 5.16: Positioning the hole

You also need to mark the starting position for the ball, so add a `Marker3D` node named `Tee` to the scene. Position it where you want the ball to start. Make sure you place it above the surface so that the ball doesn't spawn inside the ground.

With that, you're finished making the first course. Take a few minutes to look around and make sure you're happy with the layout. Remember, this shouldn't be a complex or challenging layout. It's going to introduce the player to the game, and you'll be using it to test that everything is working correctly later. To do that, you next need to create the golf ball.

Making the ball

Since the ball needs physics – gravity, friction, collision with walls, and so on – `RigidBody3D` will be the best choice of node. Rigid bodies work similarly in 3D to the ones you've used before in 2D, and you'll use the same methods to interact with them, such as `_integrate_forces()` and `apply_impulse()`.

Create a new scene with a `RigidBody3D` node named `Ball` and save it.

Since you need a simple sphere shape and Godot includes primitive shapes, there's no need for a fancy 3D model here. Add a `MeshInstance3D` child and choose **New SphereMesh** for the **Mesh** property in the Inspector.

The default size is much too large, so click on the **Mesh** property to expand it and set **Radius** to `0.05` and **Height** to `0.1`.

Add a `CollisionShape3D` node and give it a `SphereShape3D`. Set its **Radius** setting to `0.05` to match the mesh.

Testing the ball

Add an instance of the `Ball` scene to your course. Position it over one of the tiles and play the scene. You should see the ball fall and land on the ground.

You can also temporarily give the ball some motion by setting the **Linear/Velocity** property. Try setting it to different values and playing the scene. Remember that the yaxis is up. Don't forget to set it back to `(0, 0, 0)` before you move on.

Improving ball collisions

You may have noticed when adjusting the velocity that the ball sometimes goes through the wall and/ or bounces oddly, especially if you choose a high-velocity value. There are several things you can do to improve the ball's behavior.

First, you can use **continuous collision detection** (**CCD**). Using CCD alters the way the physics engine calculates collisions. Normally, the engine operates by first moving the object and then testing for and resolving collisions. This is fast and works for most common situations. When using CCD, the engine projects the object's movement along its path and attempts to predict where the collision may occur. This is slower (computationally) than the default behavior, especially when simulating many objects, but it is much more accurate. Since you only have one ball in a very small environment, CCD is a good option because it won't introduce any noticeable performance penalty. You can find it in the Inspector as **Continuous CD**:

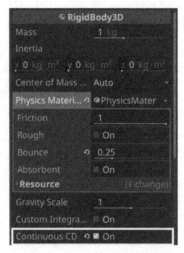

Figure 5.17: The CCD toggle

The ball also needs a little more action, so in the **Physics Material** property, choose **New** and set the **Bounce** value to 0.25. This property determines how "bouncy" a collision will be. The value can range from 0 (no bounce at all) to 1.0 (the bounciest):

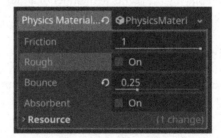

Figure 5.18: Physics material bounce settings

You may also have noticed that the ball takes a long time to come to a complete stop. Set the **Linear/Damp** property to 0.5 and **Angular/Damp** to 1. These values can be thought of as analogous to air resistance – causing the object to slow down regardless of interaction with the surface. Increasing these means the player won't have to wait as long for the ball to stop moving, and it won't appear to be spinning in place after it stops rolling.

You're finished setting up the ball, but here's another good place to pause and make sure you have everything the way you want it before moving on. Does the ball feel like it's bouncing and rolling convincingly? When it hits a wall, does it bounce too much or too little? When you've adjusted the ball's behavior to your satisfaction, move on to the next section, where you'll set up how to launch the ball.

Adding UI

Now that the ball is on the course, you need a way to aim and hit it. There are many possible control schemes for this type of game. For this project, you'll use a two-step process:

1. **Aim**: An arrow appears, swinging back and forth. Clicking the mouse button sets the aim direction.
2. **Shoot**: A power bar moves up and down. Clicking the mouse sets the power and launches the ball.

Aiming the arrow

Drawing an object in 3D is not as easy as it is in 2D. In many cases, you'll have to switch to a 3D modeling program such as Blender to create your game's objects. However, in this case, Godot's primitives will do fine. To make an arrow, you need two meshes: a long thin rectangle and a triangular prism.

> **Making your own model**
>
> If you're comfortable using a separate 3D modeling program such as *Blender*, feel free to use that to create the arrow mesh instead of following the following procedure. Just drop the exported model into your Godot project folder and load it with a `MeshInstance3D` node. See the last chapter for details about importing models directly from Blender.

Start a new scene by adding a `Node3D` node called `Arrow` and give it a `MeshInstance3D` child. Give this mesh a `BoxMesh` function and set the box's **Size** setting to `(0.5, 0.2, 2)`. This will be the body of the arrow, but before moving on, there is a problem. If you rotate the parent node, the mesh rotates around its center. You need it to rotate around its end, so change the **Position** setting of the `MeshInstance3D` node to `(0, 0, -1)`. Remember, this property is measured relative to the node's parent, so this is offsetting the mesh from the `Node3D` node:

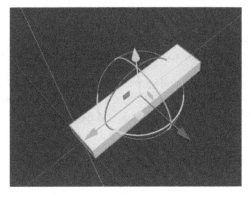

Figure 5.19: Offsetting the base

Try rotating the root node (Arrow) with the gizmo to confirm that the shape is now offset correctly.

When it's viewed in the game, the arrow should be semi-transparent. You can also give it a color to make it stand out more. To change a mesh's visual properties, you need to use **Material**.

Under the mesh properties (where you set the size), you'll see a **Material** property that's currently empty. Click the arrow to create a new StandardMaterial3D node in this box:

Figure 5.20: Offsetting the base

If you click this new material object to expand it, you'll see a long list of new properties. Don't worry, there are only two that you need to change.

First, expand the **Transparency** section and set **Transparency** to **Alpha**. This property tells the rendering engine that this object can allow light to pass through it.

Next, the color of an object is set in the **Albedo** section. Click the **Color** property and choose a yellowish color. Make sure to set the **Alpha** value to something around the middle, such as 128.

Now, to create the pointy end of the arrow, add another MeshInstance3D node, and this time, choose a PrismMesh mesh. Set its **Size** setting to (1.5, 1.5, 0.2) so that you have a flat triangular shape. To place it at the end of the rectangle, change its **Position** setting to (0, 0, -2.75) and its **Rotation** setting to (-90, 0, 0).

Finally, scale the whole arrow down by setting the root node's **Scale** setting to (0.25, 0.25, 0.25).

You also need to set the prism's material just as you did with the other section. To do this quickly, select the box shape and find its material property again. In the dropdown for the material, choose **Copy**. You can then go to the prism mesh and paste the same material onto it. Note that since they have the same material, any change you make to one shape will apply to both shapes:

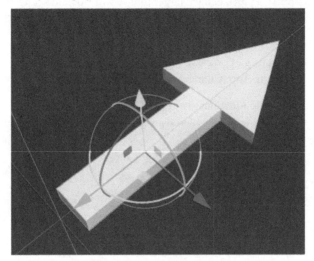

Figure 5.21: Positioning the arrow

Your aiming arrow is complete. Save the scene and instance it into your `Hole` scene.

UI display

Create a new scene using a `CanvasLayer` layer named `UI`. In this scene, you'll show the power bar as well as the shot count for the player's score. Just as it did in 2D, this node will cause its contents to be drawn above the main scene.

Add a `Label` node, then a `MarginContainer` node. In that, add a `VboxContainer` node, and in that, two `Label` nodes and a `TextureProgressBar` node. Name them as shown:

Figure 5.22: The UI node layout

In the `MarginContainer` section, set **Theme Overrides/Constants** to 20. Add the `Xolonium-Regular.ttf` font to both of the `Label` nodes and set their font sizes to 30. Set the **Text** setting of `Shots` to **Shots: 0** and `PowerLabel` to **Power**.

Add the font for the `Message` label, using a larger font size of 80, and set its text to `Get Ready!`. Choose **Center** from the **Anchor Presets** menu, then click the eye symbol next to the message to hide it.

Drag one of the colored bar textures from `res://assets` into the **Texture/Progress** section of `PowerBar`. By default, `TextureProgressBar` grows from left to right, so for a vertical orientation, change **Fill Mode** to **Bottom to Top**. Change **Value** to a few different values to see the result.

The completed UI layout should look like this:

Figure 5.23: The UI preview

Add an instance of `UI` in the `Hole` scene. Because it's `CanvasLayer`, it will be drawn on top of the 3D camera view.

Now that you've finished drawing the course and you've added the UI, you have all of the visual elements that the player will see while playing. Your next task will be to make these parts work together by adding some code.

Scripting the game

In this section, you'll create the scripts needed to make everything work together. The flow of the game will be as follows:

1. Place the ball at the `Tee`.

2. Switch to **Aim** mode and animate the arrow until the player clicks.

3.   Switch to **Power** mode and animate the power bar until the player clicks.

4.   Launch the ball.

5.   Repeat the process from *step 2* until the ball falls into the hole.

UI code

Add this script to the UI instance to update the UI elements:

```
extends CanvasLayer

@onready var power_bar = $MarginContainer/VBoxContainer/PowerBar
@onready var shots = $MarginContainer/VBoxContainer/Shots

var bar_textures = {
    "green": preload("res://assets/bar_green.png"),
    "yellow": preload("res://assets/bar_yellow.png"),
    "red": preload("res://assets/bar_red.png")
}

func update_shots(value):
    shots.text = "Shots: %s" % value

func update_power_bar(value):
    power_bar.texture_progress = bar_textures["green"]
    if value > 70:
        power_bar.texture_progress = bar_textures["red"]
    elif value > 40:
        power_bar.texture_progress = bar_textures["yellow"]
    power_bar.value = value
func show_message(text):
    $Message.text = text
    $Message.show()
    await get_tree().create_timer(2).timeout
    $Message.hide()
```

These functions provide a way to update the UI elements when they need to display a new value. As you did in *Space Rocks*, changing the progress bar's texture based on its value gives a nice low/medium/high feel to the power level.

Main script

Add a script to the Hole scene and start with these variables:

```
extends Node3D

enum {AIM, SET_POWER, SHOOT, WIN}

@export var power_speed = 100
@export var angle_speed = 1.1

var angle_change = 1
var power = 0
var power_change = 1
var shots = 0
var state = AIM
```

The enum lists the states the game can be in, while the power and angle variables will be used to set their respective values and change them over time. You can control the animation speed (and therefore the difficulty) by adjusting the two exported variables.

Next, set the initial values before starting to play:

```
func _ready():
    $Arrow.hide()
    $Ball.position = $Tee.position
    change_state(AIM)
    $UI.show_message("Get Ready!")
```

The ball gets moved to the tee position, and you change to the AIM state to begin.

Here's what needs to happen for each game state:

```
func change_state(new_state):
    state = new_state
    match state:
        AIM:
            $Arrow.position = $Ball.position
            $Arrow.show()
        SET_POWER:
            power = 0
        SHOOT:
            $Arrow.hide()
            $Ball.shoot($Arrow.rotation.y, power / 15)
            shots += 1
            $UI.update_shots(shots)
```

```
WIN:
    $Ball.hide()
    $Arrow.hide()
    $UI.show_message("Win!")
```

AIM places the aiming arrow at the ball's position and makes it visible. Recall that you offset the arrow, so it will appear to be pointing out from the ball. When you rotate the arrow, you'll rotate it around the y axis so that it remains parallel to the ground.

Also, note that when entering the SHOOT state, you call the shoot() function on the ball, which you haven't defined yet. You'll add that in the next section.

The next step is to check for user input:

```
func _input(event):
    if event.is_action_pressed("click"):
        match state:
            AIM:
                change_state(SET_POWER)
            SET_POWER:
                change_state(SHOOT)
```

The only input for the game (so far) is clicking the left mouse button. Depending on what state you're currently in, clicking it will transition to the next state.

In _process(), you'll determine what to animate based on the state. For now, it just calls the function that animates the appropriate property:

```
func _process(delta):
    match state:
        AIM:
            animate_arrow(delta)
        SET_POWER:
            animate_power(delta)
        SHOOT:
            pass
```

Both of these functions are similar. They gradually change a value between two extremes, reversing direction when the limit is reached. Note that the arrow is animating over a 180° range (+90° to -90°):

```
func animate_arrow(delta):
    $Arrow.rotation.y += angle_speed * angle_change * delta
    if $Arrow.rotation.y > PI / 2:
        angle_change = -1
    if $Arrow.rotation.y < -PI / 2:
        angle_change = 1
```

```
func animate_power(delta):
    power += power_speed * power_change * delta
    if power >= 100:
        power_change = -1
    if power <= 0:
        power_change = 1
    $UI.update_power_bar(power)
```

To detect when the ball drops into the hole, select the Area3D node that you positioned at the hole and connect its body_entered signal:

```
func _on_hole_body_entered(body):
    if body.name == "Ball":
        print("win!")
        change_state(WIN)
```

Lastly, the player will need to be able to start the whole process again after the ball comes to a stop.

Ball script

In the ball's script, there are two functions needed. First, an *impulse* must be applied to the ball to start it moving. Second, when the ball stops moving, it needs to notify the main scene so that the player can take the next shot.

Make sure you add this script to the Ball scene, not the instance of the ball in the Hole scene:

```
extends RigidBody3D

signal stopped

func shoot(angle, power):
    var force = Vector3.FORWARD.rotated(Vector3.UP, angle)
    apply_central_impulse(force * power)

func _integrate_forces(state):
    if state.linear_velocity.length() < 0.1:
        stopped.emit()
        state.linear_velocity = Vector3.ZERO
    if position.y < -20:
        get_tree().reload_current_scene()
```

As you saw in the *Space Rocks* game, you can use the physics state in _integrate_forces() to safely stop the ball if the speed has gotten very low. Due to floating point issues, the velocity may not slow to 0 on its own. Its linear_velocity value may be something like 0.00000001 for quite some time after it appears to stop. Rather than wait, you can just stop the ball if the speed falls below 0.1.

There's also the chance that the ball happens to bounce over the wall and fall off the course. If this happens, you can reload the scene to let the player start over.

Go back to the Hole scene and connect the Ball instance's stopped signal:

```
func _on_ball_stopped():
    if state == SHOOT:
        change_state(AIM)
```

Testing it out

Try playing the scene. You should see the arrow rotating at the ball's position. When you click the mouse button, the arrow stops, and the power bar starts moving up and down. When you click again, the ball is launched.

If any of those steps don't work, don't go any further. Go back and try to find what you missed in the previous section.

Once everything is working, you'll notice some areas that need improvement. First, when the ball stops moving, the arrow may not point in the direction you want. The reason for this is that the starting angle is always 0, which points along the zaxis, and then the arrow swings +/-90° from there. In the next two sections, you'll have a choice of two options for how to improve the aiming.

Option 1 for improving aiming

Aiming can be improved by pointing the 180° arc directly toward the hole at the beginning.

Add a variable called hole_dir to the top of the script. You can find this direction by using some vector math:

```
func set_start_angle():
    var hole_position = Vector2($Hole.position.z,
        $Hole.position.x)
    var ball_position = Vector2($Ball.position.z,
        $Ball.position.x)
    hole_dir = (ball_position - hole_position).angle()
    $Arrow.rotation.y = hole_dir
```

Remember that the ball's position is its center, so it's slightly above the surface, while the hole's center is a bit below it. Because of this, a vector pointing from the ball to the hole would also point at a downward angle into the ground. To prevent this and keep the arrow level, you can use only the x and z values from the position to produce Vector2.

Now, the initial angle can be set when starting the AIM state:

```
func change_state(new_state):
    state = new_state
    match state:
        AIM:
            $Arrow.position = $Ball.position
            $Arrow.show()
            set_start_angle()
```

And the animation of the arrow can use that initial direction as the basis for the +/-90° swing:

```
func animate_arrow(delta):
    $Arrow.rotation.y += angle_speed * angle_change * delta
    if $Arrow.rotation.y > hole_dir + PI / 2:
        angle_change = -1
    if $Arrow.rotation.y < hole_dir - PI / 2:
        angle_change = 1
```

Try playing again. The arrow should now always point in the general direction of the hole. This is better, but you still may have a difficult time aiming.

Option 2 for improving aiming

If you'd prefer to have more control over your aiming, then instead of animating the arrow and clicking to set the aim, you could directly control the arrow by moving the mouse side-to-side.

To accomplish this, you can make use of one of Godot's InputEvent types: InputEventMouseMotion. This event occurs whenever the mouse moves, and it includes a relative property representing how far the mouse moved in the previous frame. You can use this value to rotate that arrow by a small amount.

First, disable the arrow animation by removing the AIM section from _process().

Add a variable so that you can control how much the arrow will rotate based on the mouse movement:

```
@export var mouse_sensitivity = 150
```

Then, write the following code to _input() to check for mouse movement and rotate the arrow:

```
func _input(event):
    if event is InputEventMouseMotion:
        if state == AIM:
            $Arrow.rotation.y -= event.relative.x / mouse_sensitivity
```

Capturing the mouse

You may have noticed that as you're moving the mouse, it can leave the game window, and when you click, you don't interact with the game anymore. Most 3D games solve this problem by *capturing* the mouse – locking the mouse to the window. When you do this, you also need to give the player a way to free the mouse so that they can close the program or click on other windows, and a way to re-capture it to come back to the game.

For this game, you'll capture the mouse at first, and then if the player presses *Esc*, free it and pause the game. Clicking in the game window will un-pause and resume.

All of this functionality is controlled through the `Input.mouse_mode` property. Then, `mouse_mode` can be set to one of the following values:

- `MOUSE_MODE_VISIBLE`: This is the default mode. The mouse is visible and free to move in and out of the window.

- `MOUSE_MODE_HIDDEN`: The mouse cursor is hidden.

- `MOUSE_MODE_CAPTURED`: The mouse is hidden and its position is locked to the window.

- `MOUSE_MODE_CONFINED`: The mouse is visible, but confined to the window.

Start by capturing the mouse in `_ready()`:

```
Input.mouse_mode = Input.MOUSE_MODE_CAPTURED
```

In `_process()`, you don't want to animate things while the mouse is released:

```
func _process(delta):
    if Input.mouse_mode == Input.MOUSE_MODE_VISIBLE:
        return
```

To release the mouse, add this condition to `_input()`:

```
if event.is_action_pressed("ui_cancel") and Input.mouse_mode == Input.
MOUSE_MODE_CAPTURED:
    Input.mouse_mode = Input.MOUSE_MODE_VISIBLE
```

Then, to re-capture the mouse when the window is clicked, add this right before `match_state`:

```
if event.is_action_pressed("click"):
    if Input.mouse_mode == Input.MOUSE_MODE_VISIBLE:
        Input.mouse_mode = Input.MOUSE_MODE_CAPTURED
        return
```

Play the scene to try it out.

Camera improvements

Another problem, especially if you have laid out a relatively large course, is that if you place your camera near the tee, it won't show the other parts of the course well, or at all. You need your camera to move, showing other parts of the course so the player can aim comfortably.

There are two main ways you could address this problem:

1. Multiple cameras: place several cameras at different locations around the course. Attach `Area3D` nodes to them, and when the ball enters a camera's area, make that camera active by setting its `current` property to `true`.

2. Moving camera: stick to having one camera, but make it move along with the ball, so the player's perspective is always based on the ball's location.

Both of these schemes have pros and cons. Option 1 requires more planning, deciding exactly where to position the cameras, and how many to use. For that reason, this section will focus on option 2.

In many 3D games, the player can control a camera that rotates and moves. Typically, this control scheme uses a combination of mouse and keyboard. Since you're already using mouse movement for aiming (if you chose that option), the *W/A/S/D* keys are a good choice. The mouse wheel can be used to control the camera's zoom.

Add these new actions in the **Input Map** property:

Figure 5.24: Input map

Creating a gimbal

The camera movement needs to have some restrictions. For one, it should always remain level and not become tilted side to side. Try this: take a camera and rotate it a small amount around y (the gizmo's green ring), then a small amount around x (the red ring). Now, reverse the y rotation and click the **Preview** button. See how the camera has become tilted?

The solution to this problem is to place the camera on a **gimbal** – a device designed to keep an object level during movement. You can create a gimbal using two Node3D nodes, which will control the camera's left/right and up/down movement respectively.

First, make sure to remove any other Camera3D nodes in the scene, so that you don't have any conflict over which camera is being used.

Create a new scene and add two Node3D nodes and a Camera3D node, naming them as shown in *Figure 5.25*:

Figure 5.25: Camera gimbal node setup

Set the **Position** setting of Camera3D to (0, 0, 10) so that it's offset and looking toward the origin.

Here's how the gimbal works: the outer node is allowed to rotate *only* in y, while the inner one rotates *only* in x. You can try it yourself, but make sure to turn on **Use Local Space** (see the *Introduction to 3D space* section). Remember to only move the *green* ring of the outer gimbal node, and only the *red* ring of the inner one. Don't change the camera at all. Reset all rotations back to zero once you've finished experimenting.

To control this motion in the game, attach a script to the root node and add the following:

```
extends Node3D

@export var cam_speed = PI / 2
@export var zoom_speed = 0.1

var zoom = 0.2

func _input(event):
    if event.is_action_pressed("cam_zoom_in"):
        zoom -= zoom_speed
    if event.is_action_pressed("cam_zoom_out"):
        zoom += zoom_speed
```

```
func _process(delta):
    zoom = clamp(zoom, 0.1, 2.0)
    scale = Vector3.ONE * zoom
    var y = Input.get_axis("cam_left", "cam_right")
    rotate_y(y * cam_speed * delta)
    var x = Input.get_axis("cam_up", "cam_down")
    $GimbalInner.rotate_x(x * cam_speed * delta)
    $GimbalInner.rotation.x = clamp($GimbalInner.rotation.x,
        -PI / 2, -0.2)
```

As you can see, the right/left actions rotate the root Node3D node around its yaxis, while the up/down actions rotate GimbalInner on its xaxis. The entire gimbal system's scale property is used to handle zooming. Finally, the rotation and zoom are limited by using clamp(), preventing the user from flipping the camera upside down or zooming too close or far away.

Add an instance of CameraGimbal to the Hole scene.

The next step is to make the camera follow the ball. You can do this in _process() by setting the camera's position to the ball's:

```
if state != WIN:
    $CameraGimbal.position = $Ball.position
```

Play the scene and test that you can rotate and zoom the camera and that it moves when the ball when you make a shot.

Designing a full course

Once the ball falls into the hole, the player should advance to play the next hole. Add this variable at the top of hole.gd:

```
@export var next_hole : PackedScene
```

This will let you set the next hole that will be loaded. In the Inspector, select the **Next Hole** property to choose what scene to load next.

Add the loading code in the WIN state:

```
WIN:
$Ball.hide()
$Arrow.hide()
    await get_tree().create_timer(1).timeout
    if next_hole:
        get_tree().change_scene_to_packed(next_hole)
```

Your `Hole` scene is intended to be the generic scaffold for building multiple holes the player can play through. Now that you have it working, you can use it to make multiple scenes using **Scene** -> **New Inherited Scene**.

Using this technique, you can make as many holes as you want and chain them together into the full golf course. Here's the second hole in the example project:

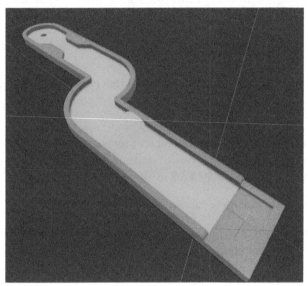

Figure 5.26: Example course layout

Visual effects

The appearance of the ball and the other meshes in your scene have been intentionally left very plain. You can think of the flat, white ball as a blank canvas, ready to be painted. First, a bit of vocabulary:

- **Textures**: Textures are flat, 2D images that are *wrapped* around 3D objects. Imagine wrapping a gift: the flat paper is folded around the package, conforming to its shape. Textures can be simple or complex, depending on the shape they're designed to be applied to.

- **Shaders**: While textures determine *what* is drawn on an object's surface, shaders determine *how* it is drawn. Imagine a wall with a texture that shows a pattern of bricks. How would it look if it were wet? The mesh and texture would be the same, but the way the light reflects from it would be quite different. This is the function of shaders – to alter the appearance of an object by altering how light interacts with it. Shaders are typically written in a specialized programming language and can use a great deal of advanced math, the details of which are beyond the scope of this book. However, Godot provides an alternative method of creating a shader for your objects that allows a great deal of customization without needing to write shader code: `StandardMaterial3D`.

- **Materials**: Godot uses a graphics rendering model called **Physically Based Rendering** (**PBR**). The goal of PBR is to render graphics in a way that accurately models the way light works in the real world. These effects are applied to meshes using their material property. Materials are essentially containers for textures and shaders. The material's properties determine how the texture and shader effects are applied. Using Godot's built-in material properties, you can simulate a wide range of physical materials, such as stone, cloth, or metal. If the built-in properties aren't enough for your purposes, you can write your own shader code to add even more effects.

Adding materials

In the `Ball` scene, select `MeshInstance` and in its **Mesh** properties find **Material** and add a new `StandardMaterial3D` node.

Expand the material and you'll see a large number of properties, far more than can be covered here. This section will focus on some of the most useful ones for making the ball look more appealing. You are encouraged to visit `https://docs.godotengine.org/en/latest/tutorials/3d/standard_material_3d.html` for a full explanation of all the settings.

To begin, try experimenting with these parameters:

- **Albedo**: This property sets the base color of the material. Change this to make the ball whatever color you'd like. If you're working with an object that needs a texture, this is where you'd add it as well.

- **Metallic and Roughness**: These parameters control how the surface reflects light. Both can be set to values between 0 and 1. The **Metallic** value controls *shininess*. Higher values will reflect more light, as with metallic substances. The **Roughness** value applies an amount of blur to the reflection. Lower values are more reflective, such as the polished surface of a mirror. You can simulate a wide variety of materials by adjusting these two properties. *Figure 5.27* is a guide to how the **Roughness** and **Metallic** properties affect the appearance of an object. Keep in mind that lighting and other factors will alter the appearance as well. Understanding how light and reflections interact with surface properties is a big part of designing effective 3D objects:

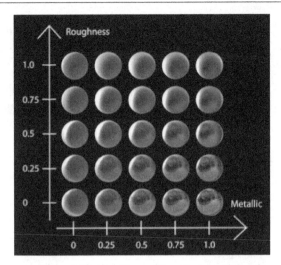

Figure 5.27: Metallic and Roughness values

- **Normal Map**: Normal mapping is a 3D graphics technique for simulating the appearance of bumps and dents on a surface. Modeling these in the mesh itself would result in a large increase in the number of polygons, or faces, making up the object, leading to reduced performance. Instead, a 2D texture is used that maps the pattern of light and shadow that would result from these small surface features. The lighting engine then uses that information to alter the reflection as if those details were actually there. A properly constructed normal map can add a great amount of detail to an otherwise bland-looking object.

The ball is a perfect example of a good use case for normal mapping because a real golf ball has hundreds of dimples on its surface, but the sphere primitive you're using is a smooth surface. Using a regular texture could add spots, but they would look flat as if they were painted on the surface. A normal map to simulate those dimples would look like this:

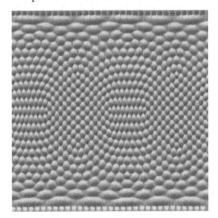

Figure 5.28: A normal map

The pattern of red and blue contains information telling the engine which direction it should assume the surface is facing at that point, and therefore which direction the light should bounce in that position. Note the stretching along the top and bottom – that's because this image is made to be wrapped around a sphere shape.

Enable the **Normal Map** property and drag `res://assets/ball_normal_map.png` into the **Texture** field. Try this with the **Albedo** color set to white at first, so you can best see the effect. Adjust the **Depth** parameter to increase or decrease the strength of the effect. A negative value will make the dimples look inset. Something between `-0.5` and `-1.0` works best:

Figure 5.29: A ball with a normal map

Take some time to experiment with these settings and find a combination you like. Don't forget to try playing the scene as well, as the ambient lighting of the `WorldEnvironment` feature will affect the final result.

In the next section, you'll learn how to adjust the `WorldEnvironment` settings to change the look of the scene.

Lighting and Environment

You've been using the default lighting setup, which you added to your scene back in the first section. While you may be happy with this lighting setup, you can also adjust it to dramatically change the appearance of your game.

The `WorldEnvironment` node contains an `Environment` property that controls the background, sky, ambient light, and other aspects of the scene's appearance. Select the node and click the property to expand it:

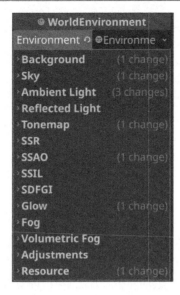

Figure 5.30: Environment properties

There are a lot of settings here, some of which are only really useful in specific advanced situations. However, these are the ones you'll find yourself using the most often:

- **Background and Sky**: Here, you can configure the background appearance of the 3D scene. You can choose a solid color or a `Sky` material. Sky materials can either be special textures that wrap around the scene (see the next game for an example) or one that's automatically generated by the engine. The default sky that you're using now is the latter: `ProceduralSkyMaterial`. Expand it to take a look at the properties – you can configure the sky's colors and the sun's appearance.

- **Ambient Light**: This is global light that affects all meshes with the same intensity. You can set its color and how much of it is generated by the sky. To see the effect, try setting the color to white and reducing the **Sky Contribution** a bit.

- **Screen Space Reflection** (SSR), **Screen Space Ambient Occlusion** (SSAO), **Screen Space Indirect Lighting** (SSIL), and **Signed Distance Field Global Illumination** (SDFGI).

These options provide more advanced control over how lighting and shadows are processed. An entire book could be written about the art of good lighting, but for the purposes of this section, you should know that each of these features introduces a tradeoff between realistic rendering and performance. Most advanced lighting features are not available at all for low-end devices, such as mobile or older PC hardware. If you'd like to learn more, the Godot documentation has an extensive introduction to the usage of these lighting features.

The **Glow** lighting feature simulates the filmic effect of light that "bleeds" into its surroundings, making objects appear to be emitting light. Note that this is different from the **Emission** property of materials, which causes objects to actually emit light. Glow is enabled by default, but at a very subtle setting that may not be apparent in bright lighting.

Feel free to experiment with the various environment settings. If you get completely lost and want to return to the default, delete the `WorldEnvironment` node, and you'll be able to add the default version back again from the menu.

Summary

This chapter introduced you to 3D development. One of Godot's great strengths is that the same tools and workflow are used in both 2D and 3D. Everything you learned about the process of creating scenes, instancing, and using signals works in the same way. For example, an interface you build with control nodes for a 2D game can be dropped into a 3D game and will work just the same.

In this chapter, you learned how to navigate the 3D editor to view and place nodes using gizmos. You learned about meshes and how to quickly make your own objects using Godot's primitives. You used `GridMap` to lay out your minigolf course. You learned about using cameras, lighting, and the world environment to design how your game will appear on the screen. Finally, you got a taste of using PBR rendering via Godot's `SpatialMaterial` resource.

In the next project, you'll continue working in 3D and extend your understanding of transforms and meshes.

6
Infinite Flyer

In this chapter, you'll build a 3D infinite runner (or more accurately, infinite *flyer*) in the vein of *Temple Run* or *Subway Surfers*. The player's goal is to fly as far as possible, passing through floating rings to collect points, while avoiding obstacles. By building this game, you'll get a feel for how to make 3D objects interact and how to generate a 3D world automatically, rather than building it piece-by-piece as you did in earlier games such as *Minigolf* or *Jungle Jump*.

Here are some of the new things you'll learn in this chapter:

- Using transforms to rotate and move in 3D space

- Load and unload "chunks" of your game world

- How to randomly generate the game environment and game objects

- Saving and loading files for persistent data storage

- Using `CharacterBody3D` and detecting collisions

When completed, the game will look like this:

Figure 6.1: Finished game screenshot

Technical requirements

Download the game assets from the following link and unzip them into your new project folder:

`https://github.com/PacktPublishing/Godot-4-Game-Development-Projects-Second-Edition/tree/main/Downloads`

You can also find the complete code for this chapter on GitHub at: `https://github.com/PacktPublishing/Godot-4-Game-Development-Projects-Second-Edition/tree/main/Chapter06%20-%20Infinite%20Flyer`

Project setup

Create a new project in Godot to get started. As you've done before, download the project assets and unzip them in the new project folder. Once you've created the project, you'll start by configuring the inputs and Godot settings needed for the game.

Inputs

You'll control the plane with up, down, left, and right inputs. You can add them in **Input Map** in the same way you've done with other projects. Name the four inputs `pitch_up`, `pitch_down`, `roll_left`, and `roll_right`. You can add the arrow keys and/or the *W*, *A*, *S*, and *D* keys to these, but if you have a game controller, you can also use a joystick for more precise control. To add joystick inputs, you can select **Joypad Axes** after pressing the + button. The values are labeled, such as **Left Stick Up**, so you can easily keep track of them:

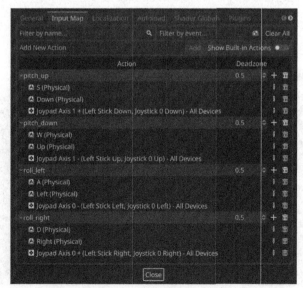

Figure 6.2: Input configuration

The nice part about this setup is that your code won't have to be any different for the different types of input. By using `Input.get_axis()` and passing in the four input events, you'll get a result whether the player pressed a key or moved the stick. Pressing the keys is equivalent to pushing the stick all the way in one direction.

Now that the project is set up, you can start making your game objects, starting with the player-controlled airplane.

Airplane scene

In this section, you'll create the airplane that the player will control. It will fly forward while the player can move it up, down, left, and right.

Start your new plane scene with a `CharacterBody3D` node named `Plane` and save it.

You can find the 3D model for the airplane in the `assets` folder, named `cartoon_plane.glb`. The name indicates the model is stored as a *binary* `.gltf` file (exported from Blender). Godot imports `.gltf` files as scenes containing meshes, animations, materials, and other objects that may have been exported in the file. Click the **Instance a Child Scene** button and choose the plane model. You'll see it appears as `Node3D`, but it's facing the wrong direction. Select it and set the **Rotation/Y** function to `180` in the Inspector feature, so that it points along the *z* axis, which is Godot's "forward" direction. Note that typing the value directly is easier than trying to rotate the node exactly using the mouse.

> **Model orientation**
>
> As mentioned in the previous chapter, the various 3D design programs use different axis orientations. It's very common to import your model and have its forward direction not match Godot's. If you're making the model yourself, you can correct this when you export it, but when you're using a model made by someone else, it's common to need to reorient it in Godot.

If you right-click on the `cartoon_plane` node and choose **Editable Children**, you'll see all of the meshes that make up the plane, plus `AnimationPlayer`:

Figure 6.3: Airplane meshes

`AnimationPlayer` contains an animation for making the propeller spin, so select it and set the `prop_spin` animation for the **Autoplay on Load** function:

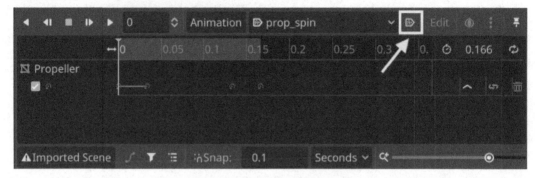

Figure 6.4: Autoplay animation

Collision shapes

Add a `CollisionShape3D` node to `Plane` and choose **New CylinderShape3D** for its **Shape** setting. You can size a cylinder with the two orange size handles, but you'll need to rotate it around the *x* axis by 90 to align it with the plane's fuselage. You can do this with the gizmo (don't forget to turn on snapping using the "Use Smart Snap" icon ▦ to get it perfectly aligned) or by typing the value directly into Inspector.

The wings also need to be covered, so add a second `CollisionShape3D` node. This time, use `BoxShape3D`. Size it to cover the wings:

Figure 6.5: Airplane collision shapes

Scripting the plane

You can begin with the airplane's controls. There are two axes of movement: "pitch up" and "pitch down" will raise or lower the nose of the plane (rotating around its *x* axis), causing it to move up or down. The `roll_left` and `roll_right` functions will rotate the plane around its *z* axis, which causes it to go left or right.

For either input, you'll want smooth rotation, and when the player lets go of the button or returns the stick to the center, the plane should smoothly rotate back to its original position. You can do this by **interpolating** the rotation rather than setting it directly when rotating.

> **About interpolation**
>
> **Linear interpolation**, typically abbreviated to **lerp**, is a term that you'll encounter often in game development. It means to calculate an intermediate value between two given values, using a straight-line function. In practice, it can be used to smoothly change a value from one value to another over time.

To begin, attach a script to the `Plane` node and define some variables:

```
extends CharacterBody3D

@export var pitch_speed = 1.1
@export var roll_speed = 2.5
@export var level_speed = 4.0

var roll_input = 0
var pitch_input = 0
```

The exported variables let you set the speed of the plane's rotation in either direction, as well as the speed of its automatic return to level flight.

In your `get_input()` function, you'll check the values of the inputs from **Input Map** to determine which way to rotate:

```
func get_input(delta):
    pitch_input = Input.get_axis("pitch_down", "pitch_up")
    roll_input = Input.get_axis("roll_left", "roll_right")
```

The `Input.get_axis()` function returns a value between -1 and 1 based on the two inputs. When using keys, which can only be pressed or not pressed, that will mean you'll only get -1 when one key is pressed, 1 for the other, and 0 when neither or both are pressed. However, when using an analog input such as a joystick axis, you can get the full range of values. This allows more precise control, as tilting the joystick only slightly to the right will give a small `roll_input` value of 0.25, for example.

In `_physics_process()`, you can then rotate the plane on its *x* axis based on the pitch input:

```
func _physics_process(delta):
    get_input(delta)

    rotation.x = lerpf(rotation.x, pitch_input,
        pitch_speed * delta)
    rotation.x = clamp(rotation.x, deg_to_rad(-45),
        deg_to_rad(45))
```

It's also important to use `clamp()` to limit the rotation so the plane doesn't flip completely upside down.

You can test this out by making a new test scene and adding the plane and `Camera3D`, like this:

Figure 6.6: Test scene

Position the camera behind the plane and run the scene to test that pressing the pitch up and pitch down inputs correctly tilts the plane up and down.

For the roll, you could rotate the body in the *z* axis as well, but then the two rotations would add together, and you'd find it very difficult to get the plane back to level flight. Since for this game, you want the plane to continue going forward, it will be easier to rotate the child mesh instead. Add this line next in `_physics_process()`:

```
$cartoon_plane.rotation.z = lerpf($cartoon_plane.rotation.z,
roll_input, roll_speed * delta)
```

Test it again in your test scene and make sure that the controls all work as expected.

To finish up the movement, add two more variables at the top of the script. Your plane's flying speed will be `forward_speed`. You'll adjust this later to change the difficulty of the game. You can use `max_altitude` to keep the plane from climbing offscreen:

```
@export var forward_speed = 25

var max_altitude = 20
```

In `get_input()`, after checking the inputs, add this to cause the plane to level out if it reaches the maximum altitude:

```
if position.y >= max_altitude and pitch_input > 0:
    position.y = max_altitude
    pitch_input = 0
```

Then, add this to _physics_process() to handle the movement. The forward velocity will be the forward_speed amount:

```
velocity = -transform.basis.z * forward_speed
```

For the side-to-side movement (in the *x* direction), you can multiply by the amount of rotation to make it faster or slower depending on how much the plane has rolled. Then, scale the speed based on the forward speed (dividing by two to make it a little bit slower – experiment here to change the feel):

```
velocity += transform.basis.x * $cartoon_plane.rotation.z / deg_to_
rad(45) * forward_speed / 2.0

move_and_slide()
```

Your plane should now be flying forward and the controls should be working as expected. Don't move on to the next step until you've checked that the plane behaves correctly. In the next section, you will build the environment for the plane to fly around in.

Building the world

Because this is an *infinite*-style game, the player will continue to fly through the world as long as possible. That means you will need to continuously create more of the world for them to see – random buildings, items to collect, and so on. It would be impractical to create this all ahead of time both because you don't know how far the player will go, and because you don't want the game to be the same every time you play. It would also be inefficient to load a huge game world if the player isn't going to see most of it.

For that reason, it makes more sense to use a **chunking** strategy. You'll randomly generate the world in smaller pieces, or chunks. You can then create these as they're needed – as the player moves forward. You can also remove them once they've been passed when the game doesn't need to keep track of them anymore.

World objects

Each time you generate a new chunk of the world, it's going to contain a number of different world objects. You can begin with two: buildings, which will be obstacles, and rings that the player tries to collect by flying through them.

Buildings

For the first building, start a new scene with a StaticBody3D node and name it Building1. Add a MeshInstance3D node and drag res://assets/building_meshes/Build_01.obj into the **Mesh** property. Rather than a .glTF file, the building's mesh is stored in the *OBJ* format. There is also a separate .mtl file that contains the mesh's material – Godot hides it in the **FileSystem** panel, but it will be used for the texture in the mesh instance.

You'll notice that the building is centered on the origin. Since your buildings are going to be of different sizes, this will make it difficult to place them all on the ground – they'll all have different offsets. If your buildings are all consistently offset ahead of time, then they can be more easily placed.

To position the building mesh, change the **Position** property of the `MeshInstance3D` node to `(0, 6, -8)`, which moves it up and places its edge on the origin. Add a collision shape by selecting the mesh and choosing **Mesh -> Create Trimesh Collision Sibling**.

Save the scene in a new folder called `res://buildings/` and repeat the process with the other buildings, starting each scene with a `StaticBody3D` node, adding the mesh, offsetting it, and then creating the collision shape. Since each building is a different size, here are the offsets that will position them perfectly:

Building	Offset
1	`(0, 6, -8)`
2	`(0, 8, -4)`
3	`(0, 10, -6)`
4	`(0, 10, -6)`
5	`(0, 11, -4)`

The chunk can now load and instance these buildings randomly to create a varied city skyline.

Rings

Rings will appear ahead of the player, and the plane needs to fly through them to score. If the plane is very close to the center of the ring, the player will get a score bonus. As the game progresses, the rings can become more difficult to catch – changing size, moving back and forth, and so on.

Before starting, and without looking ahead, think about which type of node would be best for the ring object.

Did you select `Area3D`? Since you want to detect when the plane flies through the ring, but not collide with it, an area's `body_entered` detection will be the ideal solution.

Start the new `Ring` scene with `Area3D` and add a `MeshInstance3D` child. For **Mesh**, choose `TorusMesh`, and in the mesh properties, set **Inner Radius** to `3.5` and **Outer Radius** to 4, so that you have a narrow ring.

Add a `CollisionShape3D` node and choose **New CylinderShape3D** for its **Shape**. This time, set the **Height** property to `.5` and **Radius** to 3.

Later, you'll want to animate the ring moving up and down. An easy way to do this will be to move the collision shape relative to the root node's position. Since you'll want the mesh to move as well, drag the mesh to make it a child of `CollisionShape3D`. Rotate the collision shape 90 degrees around *x* to make it stand up.

A plain white ring is not very exciting, so you can add texture. In the **Mesh** property of `MeshInstance3D`, add **New StandardMaterial3D** and click to expand it. Under **Albedo/Texture**, add `res://assets/textures/texture_09.png`. You'll notice that the texture, which is a grid of alternating light and dark squares, looks very stretched around the torus. You can adjust how a texture is wrapped around the mesh by changing the **UV1/Scale** values. Try `(12, 1, 1)` for a beginning value and adjust it to your liking. Under **Shading**, set **Shading Mode** to **Unshaded** – this will ensure that the ring ignores lighting and shadows, keeping it bright and visible at all times.

Next, add a `Label3D` node to the `Ring` node. You'll use this to show the player how many points they scored for the ring and whether or not they got the center bonus. Set the **Text/Text** field to `100` so you can see something to test. Under **Text/Font**, add `Baloo2-Medium.ttf` from the assets folder and set the font size to `720`. To make the text always face the camera, set **Flags/Billboard** to **Enabled**.

Add a script to the ring and connect the `body_entered` signal. The `Label3D` function should be hidden at first, and the ring will be hidden when the plane touches it. There's a problem, though: what if a ring spawns and overlaps a building? The `body_entered` signal will still be triggered, but you don't want the building to collect the ring!

You can solve this by setting collision layers. On the `Plane` scene, change its **Collision/Layer** value to `2` (removing `1`), then come back to the `Ring` node and set its **Collision/Mask** setting to only layer 2. Now, you can be sure that if the ring sees a body enter, it can only be the plane:

```
extends Area3D

func _ready():
    $Label3D.hide()
```

After that, you need to find the distance from the plane to the center of the ring to see if the player scored the bonus and set the `text` property to the correct value. If the plane hits the ring directly in the center (closer than 2.0 units), you can also color the text yellow to indicate the perfect hit:

```
func _on_body_entered(body):
    $CollisionShape3D/MeshInstance3D.hide()
    var d = global_position.distance_to(body.global_position)
    if d < 2.0:
        $Label3D.text = "200"
        $Label3D.modulate = Color(1, 1, 0)
    elif d > 3.5:
        $Label3D.text = "50"
```

```
else:
    $Label3D.text = "100"
$Label3D.show()
```

Continuing the _on_body_entered() function, add some animation to the label to make it move and fade out:

```
var tween = create_tween().set_parallel()
tween.tween_property($Label3D, "position",
    Vector3(0, 10, 0), 1.0)
tween.tween_property($Label3D, "modulate:a", 0.0, 0.5)
```

Lastly, give the ring a nice rotation effect:

```
func _process(delta):
    $CollisionShape3D/MeshInstance3D.rotate_y(deg_to_rad(50) * delta)
```

Chunks

Now that you've got the building blocks of your chunk, you can make the chunk scene itself. This is the scene that the game will instance whenever there needs to be more of the world ahead of the player. When you instantiate a new chunk, it will randomly place buildings along the left and right sides, as well as spawning rings at random points along its length.

Start the Chunk scene with a Node3D node and a MeshInstance3D child named Ground. Make the **Mesh** property a PlaneMesh and set its **Size** setting to (50, 200). This is the size of a single chunk:

Figure 6.7: Plane size settings

Position it to start at the origin by setting its **Z** position to `-100`:

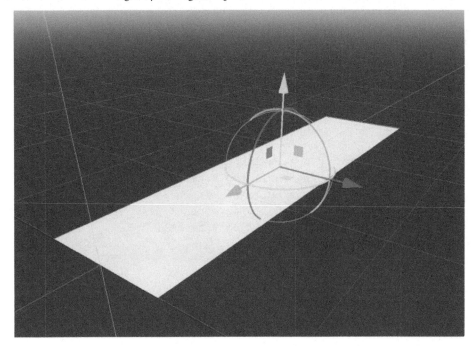

Figure 6.8: Positioning the plane

Add material and use `texture_01.png` as the **Albedo/Texture** and set the **UV1/Scale** values to `(2, 10, 2)`. By default, Godot links the three scale values to keep them the same, so you'll need to uncheck the link button to allow them to be different:

Figure 6.9: Adjusting the UV scale

Select the `Ground` node and choose **Mesh -> Create Trimesh Static Body** to add a `StaticBody3D` node and a `CollisionShape3D` node that matches the size of the ground.

As the plane moves toward the end of the chunk, you'll spawn a new chunk ahead, and you can also remove old chunks once they've passed by. To assist with the latter, add a `VisibleOnScreenNotifier3D` node and set its **Position** property to `(0, 0, -250)`, which places it past the end of the ground plane.

You can now add a script to the Chunk node and connect the notifier's `screen_exited` signal so that the chunk will be removed:

```
func _on_visible_on_screen_notifier_3d_screen_exited():
    queue_free()
```

At the top of the script, load the scenes that need to be instanced:

```
extends Node3D

var buildings = [
    preload("res://buildings/building_1.tscn"),
    preload("res://buildings/building_2.tscn"),
    preload("res://buildings/building_3.tscn"),
    preload("res://buildings/building_4.tscn"),
    preload("res://buildings/building_5.tscn"),
]
var ring = preload("res://ring.tscn")

var level = 0
```

> **Loading many scenes**
>
> In a bigger game, where you have a much larger number of buildings and possibly other scenes, you wouldn't want to write them all out individually in the script as you've done here. Another solution would be to write code here that loads every scene file saved in a particular folder.

The `level` variable can be set by the main scene when the chunk is loaded to allow increasing difficulty by spawning rings with different behaviors (more about that later).

In `_ready()`, the chunk needs to do three things:

- Spawn buildings along the sides of the ground plane
- Occasionally spawn buildings in the middle to act as obstacles
- Spawn rings

Each of these steps will involve some code, so you can keep it all organized by creating three separate functions:

```
func _ready():
    add_buildings()
    add_center_buildings()
    add_rings()
```

The first step is to spawn the side buildings. Since they need to be on both sides of the chunk, you repeat the loop twice – once for the positive *x* direction and once for the negative direction. Each time, you'll move along the length of the chunk spawning random buildings:

```
func add_buildings():
    for side in [-1, 1]:
        var zpos = -10
        for i in 18:
            if randf() > 0.75:
                zpos -= randi_range(5, 10)
                continue
            var nb = buildings[randi_range(0,
                buildings.size()-1)].instantiate()
            add_child(nb)
            nb.transform.origin.z = zpos
            nb.transform.origin.x = 20 * side
            zpos -= nb.get_node("MeshInstance3D").mesh.get_aabb().size.z
```

The randf() function is a common random function that returns a floating point number between 0 and 1, making it easy to use to calculate percentages. Check here if the random number is greater than 0.75 to have a 25% chance of there being no building at a particular spot.

By getting the size of the building mesh using get_aabb(), you can ensure that the buildings don't overlap each other. The position of the next building will be exactly at the edge of the previous one.

Next, spawning middle buildings won't happen at the start, but later in the game, they'll start appearing with a 20% probability:

```
func add_center_buildings():
    if level > 0:
        for z in range(0, -200, -20):
            if randf() > 0.8:
                var nb = buildings[0].instantiate()
                add_child(nb)
                nb.position.z = z
                nb.position.x += 8
                nb.rotation.y = PI / 2
```

The third step is spawning the rings. Right now, it just positions some rings at random fixed positions. Later, you'll add some more variation here as the game progresses:

```
func add_rings():
    for z in range(0, -200, -10):
        if randf() > 0.76:
            var nr = ring.instantiate()
```

```
nr.position.z = z
nr.position.y = randf_range(3, 17)
add_child(nr)
```

You're finished setting up the chunk. When it loads, it takes care of populating itself with a random assortment of buildings and rings, and it also removes itself when it later goes offscreen. In the next section, you'll bring it all together in a scene that instantiates chunks as the plane moves forward.

Main scene

In this section, you'll make the main scene, which, in this game, will handle loading the world chunks, displaying the game information, and starting and ending the game.

Start a new scene with a `Node3D` named `Main`. Add an instance of the `Plane` and an instance of the `Chunk` to start with.

You'll also need some lighting, so in the toolbar, choose the "Edit Sun and Environment settings" dropdown and add the sun and environment to the scene:

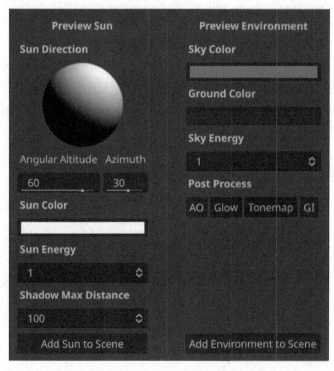

Figure 6.10: Add environment and sun

Rather than use the generated sky texture, you can use `styled_sky.hdr` found in the assets folder. Select `WorldEnvironment` and then expand its **Sky** property. You'll see that it's set to `ProdeduralSkyMaterial`. Click the down arrow and choose **New PanoramaSkyMaterial**. When you expand that, you'll see an empty **Panorama** property where you can drag and drop `styled_sky.hdr`:

Figure 6.11: WorldEnvironment sky settings

Before you can test, you'll also need a camera. Add a `Camera3D` and then add a script to it. Since it's a standalone node without any children, you don't need to make it a separate saved scene:

```
extends Camera3D

@export var target_path : NodePath
@export var offset = Vector3.ZERO

var target = null

func _ready():
    if target_path:
```

```
        target = get_node(target_path)
        position = target.position + offset
        look_at(target.position)

func _physics_process(_delta):
    if !target:
        return
    position = target.position + offset
```

This camera script is generic and could be used in other projects where you want a camera to follow a moving 3D object.

Select the Camera3D node and in Inspector, click **Target Path** and choose the Plane node. Set **Offset** to (7, 7, 15), which will keep the camera behind, above, and to the right of the plane.

Figure 6.12: Camera follow settings

Play the Main scene and you should be able to fly along the chunk, collecting rings. If you run into the buildings, nothing will happen, and when you reach the end of the chunk, you won't see another one.

Spawning new chunks

The length of each chunk is 200, so when the plane has traveled half that distance, a new chunk should spawn ahead at the end position of the previous chunk. The max_position setting will keep track of the middle of the next chunk ahead, which is the position that the plane needs to reach to spawn a new chunk.

You'll also keep track of how many chunks have been spawned, so you can use that to determine when the game should get harder.

Add a script to Main and add the following:

```
extends Node3D

var chunk = preload("res://chunk.tscn")

var num_chunks = 1
var chunk_size = 200
var max_position = -100
```

Remember that everything is moving forward in the -z direction, so the position at the center of the first chunk will have a z value of -100. The plane's z coordinate will continue to decrease as it moves forward.

In _process(), you'll check the plane's position, and if it goes past max_position, it's time to instantiate a new chunk and update max_position to the center of the next chunk:

```
func _process(delta):
    if $Plane.position.z  < max_position:
        num_chunks += 1
        var new_chunk = chunk.instantiate()
        new_chunk.position.z = max_position - chunk_size / 2
        new_chunk.level = num_chunks / 4
        add_child(new_chunk)
        max_position -= chunk_size
```

Here is where the chunk spawning happens. The new chunk gets placed at the end of the previous one. Remember that max_position is the center of the chunk, so you also need to add chunk_size / 2.

Then, to get the level number, dividing by 4 results in **integer division**, meaning the fractional part will be discarded. For example, on chunk number 5, 5/4 is just 1. The level will reach 2 at chunk number 8, 3 at chunk number 12, and so on. This will give you a gradual increase in difficulty.

Play the scene. You should now see the new chunks appearing ahead of the plane as it moves forward.

Increasing difficulty

Now that you're spawning chunks, they're being given a level value that gradually increases. You can use that to start making the rings more challenging to collect. For example, currently, they're placed exactly in the center, so the player doesn't need to steer left or right at all. You could start randomizing the x coordinate of the rings. You could also start making the rings move back and forth or up and down.

Add these variables to the top of ring.gd:

```
var move_x = false
var move_y = false

var move_amount = 2.5
var move_speed = 2.0
```

The two Boolean variables will let you turn on movement in the x or y direction, and move_amount and move_speed will let you control how much movement you want.

When those values are set, you can check `_ready()`, start the movement, then use a tween:

```
func _ready():
    $Label3D.hide()
    var tween = create_tween().set_loops()
        .set_trans(Tween.TRANS_SINE)
    tween.stop()
    if move_y:
        tween.tween_property($CollisionShape3D,
            "position:y", -move_amount, move_speed)
        tween.tween_property($CollisionShape3D,
            "position:y", move_amount, move_speed)
        tween.play()
    if move_x:
        tween.tween_property($CollisionShape3D,
            "position:x", -move_amount, move_speed)
        tween.tween_property($CollisionShape3D,
            "position:x", move_amount, move_speed)
        tween.play()
```

Note that by default, a tween starts playing automatically. Since you may or may not be actually animating a property, depending on what level the player is on, you can use `stop()` to stop the tween initially and then use `play()` to start it once you've set up which property you want to affect. By using `set_loops()`, you're telling the tween to repeat the two moves endlessly, moving back and forth.

Now the ring is ready to move, your chunk can set these values when it spawns the ring. Go to `chunk.gd` and update the section that spawns rings to use `level`:

```
func add_rings():
    for z in range(0, -200, -10):
        var n = randf()
        if n > 0.76:
            var nr = ring.instantiate()
            nr.position.z = z
            nr.position.y = randf_range(3, 17)
            match level:
                0: pass
                1:
                    nr.move_y = true
                2:
                    nr.position.x = randf_range(-10, 10)
                    nr.move_y = true
                3:
                    nr.position.x = randf_range(-10, 10)
```

```
                        nr.move_x = true
            add_child(nr)
```

As you can see, once the level reaches 1, the rings will start moving up and down. At level 2, they'll start to have a random *x* position, and at level 3, they'll start moving horizontally.

You should consider this an example of what's possible. Feel free to create your own pattern of increasing difficulty.

Collisions

The next step is to make the plane explode if it runs into anything, such as the ground or the buildings. If it does, you'll play an explosion animation, and that's the end of the game.

Explosion

Go to your `Plane` scene and add an `AnimatedSprite3D` child. Name it `Explosion`.

The `AnimatedSprite3D` node works very much like the 2D version you used earlier in the book. Add a new `SpriteFrames` resource in the **Frames** property, and click it to open the **SpriteFrames** panel at the bottom of the screen. Drag the five images from `res://assets/smoke/` into the **Animation Frames** box, set **Speed** to 10 FPS, and turn off **Loop**:

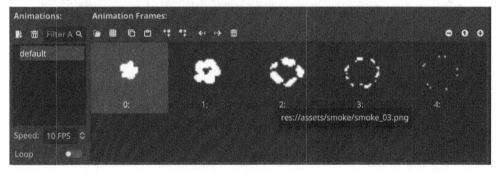

Figure 6.13: Explosion sprite frames

You may notice that you can't see the sprite in the viewport. When displaying a 2D image, which is drawn in pixels, in 3D, the engine needs to know how big a pixel is in 3D space. To size the explosion to match the size of the plane, set **Pixel Size** to 0.5 in Inspector. Under **Flags**, set **Billboard** to enabled. This ensures that the sprite always faces the camera. You should now see a large cloud (the first frame of the animation) superimposed on your plane.

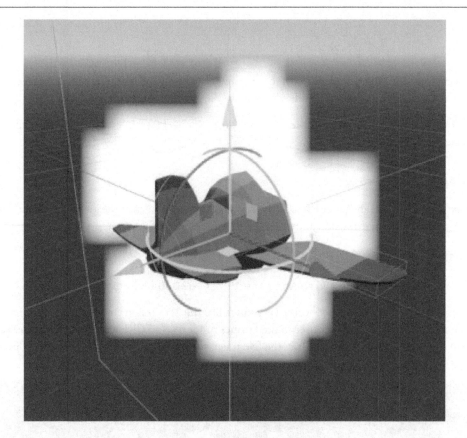

Figure 6.14: Explosion sprite

You don't want to see the explosion, so click the eye icon to hide Explosion.

Scripting the collisions

Add a new signal at the top of plane.gd, which will notify the game that the player has crashed:

```
signal dead
```

In _physics_process(), you're using move_and_slide() to move the plane. Whenever a CharacterBody3D node is moved with this method, it can check for **slide collisions**. Since it doesn't matter *what* the plane collided with, only that there *was* a collision, add this just after move_and_slide():

```
if get_slide_collision_count() > 0:
    die()
```

You can then define the `die()` function to handle what should happen when the plane crashes. First, it will stop moving forward. Then, you can hide the plane and show the explosion, playing the animation. Once the animation has ended, you can reset the game. Since you haven't made the title screen yet, you can just restart for now:

```
func die():
    set_physics_process(false)
    $cartoon_plane.hide()
    $Explosion.show()
    $Explosion.play("default")
    await $Explosion.animation_finished
    $Explosion.hide()
    dead.emit()
    get_tree().reload_current_scene()
```

You'll remove that last line later once the rest of the game has been set up.

Play the `Main` scene now and try running into something to verify that the explosion plays and the scene restarts.

Fuel and score

The next step is to keep track of the score earned when collecting the rings. You'll also add a fuel component to the plane. This value will steadily decrease, and the game will end if the fuel runs out. The player gets fuel back based on collecting the rings.

Add two new signals at the top of `plane.gd`:

```
signal score_changed
signal fuel_changed
```

These will notify the UI to display the score and fuel values.

Then, add these new variables:

```
@export var fuel_burn = 1.0
var max_fuel = 10.0
var fuel = 10.0:
    set = set_fuel
var score = 0:
    set = set_score
```

The setter functions for these variables will update them and emit the signals:

```
func set_fuel(value):
    fuel = min(value, max_fuel)
```

```
        fuel_changed.emit(fuel)
        if fuel <= 0:
            die()

    func set_score(value):
        score = value
        score_changed.emit(score)
```

To reduce the fuel over time, add this line to _physics_process():

```
fuel -= fuel_burn * delta
```

Try playing the main scene and you'll see that you run out of fuel and explode after about 10 seconds.

Now, you can make the rings update the score and give some fuel back based on how close the player was to the center of the ring. You're already setting the ring's label, and you can do the rest in the same section of ring.gd:

```
if d < 2.0:
    $Label3D.text = "200"
    $Label3D.modulate = Color(1, 1, 0)
    body.fuel = 10
    body.score += 200
elif d > 3.5:
    $Label3D.text = "50"
    body.fuel += 1
    body.score += 50
else:
    $Label3D.text = "100"
    body.fuel += 2.5
    body.score += 100
```

If you test again, you should be able to fly longer as long as you keep collecting rings. It's hard to tell how much fuel you have left, though, so you should add a UI overlay that displays the fuel and the score.

UI

Create a new scene with a CanvasLayer layer called "UI". Add two children: TextureProgressBar (FuelBar) and Label (Score).

Set the text in the Score box **Text** property to 0 and add the font as you've done before, setting its **Size** to 48. Use the toolbar menu to set the layout to **Top Right**.

For `FuelBar`, you have two textures in the `assets` folder. You can use `bar_red.png` for the **Progress** texture and `bar_glass.png` for the **Over** texture. Under **Range**, set **Max Value** to `10` and **Step** to `0.01`.

You can position the bar in the bottom left, but if you want to resize it, you'll need to change a few more settings. Check the box labeled **Nine Patch Stretch** in Inspector. You can then resize the bar by dragging its bounding box. However, you'll notice that the outline becomes very distorted – scale it very large to see the effect. To prevent this, keeping the borders unsized while stretching the interior, is what **nine patch stretch** does. Under **Stretch Margin**, set all four values to 6. You'll see that now, no matter how you resize the bar, the borders remain unstretched:

Figure 6.15: Nine patch stretch settings

Make the bar a comfortable size and then add a script to `UI`:

```
extends CanvasLayer

func update_fuel(value):
    $FuelBar.value = value

func update_score(value):
    $Score.text = str(value)
```

Add an instance of the UI scene to `Main`. Connect the plane's `score_changed` signal and the `fuel_changed` signal to the functions you just made on the UI:

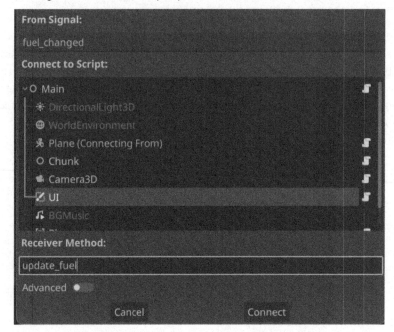

Figure 6.16: Connecting the plane's signal to the UI

Play the scene once again and verify that the bar shows the fuel changing and that the score updates correctly when rings are collected.

You are almost done! You have a mostly working game at this point. Take a moment to play it a few times to make sure you're not missing any of the interactions. Are the chunks increasing in difficulty as you fly farther? You should see moving rings and then rings that spawn to the left and right of the center. Make sure to review the previous sections if there's anything you are unclear about. When you're ready, move on to making the title screen.

Title screen

The purpose of the title screen is to introduce the game and give a way to start it by pressing a button. This section will not go into much detail on the styling – you should experiment with the settings and try to make it look pleasing.

Start your `TitleScreen` scene with a `Control` node and add a `Label` and a `TextureButton` plus a `TextureRect` for the background.

You can use `styled_sky.hdr` for the `TextureRect`'s **Texture** property. It's a lot bigger than the screen size, so feel free to scale and/or position it as you like.

For `TextureButton`, there are three images in the `res://assets/buttons/` folder for the **Normal**, **Pressed**, and **Hover** textures. The images are quite large to allow for sizing, so you can check **Ignore Texture Size** and set **Stretch Mode** to **Keep Aspect** to allow you to resize it.

The `Label` node is there to display the game's title. Set up the font with large font size, such as `128`. Arrange `Label` and `TextureButton` on the screen. Set both of their layouts to **Center** and then move them up and down to position them.

The only code needed is to determine what to do when the button is pressed, so add a script to the scene and connect the button's `pressed` signal. When the button is pressed, it should load the main scene:

```
extends Control

func _on_texture_button_pressed():
    get_tree().change_scene_to_file("res://main.tscn")
```

To return to the title screen at the end of the game, remove `get_tree().reload_current_scene()` from the plane's `die()` function, and then go to the `Main` scene and connect the plane instance's dead signal:

```
var title_screen = "res://title_screen.tscn"
func _on_plane_dead():
    get_tree(). change_scene_to_file(title_screen)
```

Now when you crash, you should immediately return to the title screen, where you can press **Play** again.

Audio

There are two sound effect files located in the `assets` folder: `impact.wav` for the plane's explosion and `three_tone.wav` for the ring collection sound. You can add `AudioStreamPlayer` nodes to the `Plane` and `Ring` scenes to play them at the appropriate time.

For the background music, which should be played in a loop during the game, add `AudioStreamPlayer` to the `Main` scene, using `Riverside Ride Short Loop.wav` for **Stream**. Since it needs to play automatically at the start, you can check the **Autoplay** box.

The audio for this game is intentionally kept simple and upbeat. While there's a sound effect for each major game event (flying through a ring, crashing), you could also try adding additional sounds for the airplane engine, bonuses, or a warning when fuel is low. Experiment to see what works for you.

Saving a high score

Saving the player's high score is another common feature in many games (and one that you can add to the other games in this book as well). Since the score needs to be saved between sessions of the game, you'll need to save it in an external file that the game can read the next time you open it.

Here's the process:

1. When the game launches, check for a save file.

2. If the save file exists, load the score from it, otherwise use 0.

3. When a game ends, check if the score is higher than the current high score. If it is, save it to the file.

4. Show the high score on the title screen.

Since you'll need to access the high score variable from different parts of your game, it makes sense to use an autoload. In the **Script** editor, click **File** -> **New Script** and name it global.gd. To begin, you'll need two variables:

```
extends Node

var high_score = 0

var score_file = "user://hs.dat"
```

About file locations

You'll notice that the path for the save file doesn't begin with res:// like all of the other files you've been working with. The res:// designation represents your game's project folder – the place where all the scripts, scenes, and assets are located. When you export your game, though, that folder becomes read-only. To store persistent data, you use a location on the device that's set aside for the game to write to: user://. Where this folder is actually located depends on the operating system you're using. For example, in Windows, it would be %APPDATA%\Godot\app_userdata\[project_name]. You can find the paths for other supported operating systems here:

https://docs.godotengine.org/en/stable/tutorials/io/data_paths.html

Accessing files

Accessing files in Godot is done via the FileAccess object. This object handles opening, reading, and writing files. Add these functions to global.gd:

```
func _ready():
    load_score()

func load_score():
    if FileAccess.file_exists(score_file):
        var file = FileAccess.open(score_file,
            FileAccess.READ)
        high_score = file.get_var()
```

```
    else:
        high_score = 0

func save_score():
    var file = FileAccess.open(score_file, FileAccess.WRITE)
    file.store_var(high_score)
```

As you can see, the script calls `load_score()` in `_ready()`, so it's done immediately when the game is launched. The `load_score()` function uses `FileAccess` to check if the save file exists, and if it does, it opens it and retrieves the data that was stored in it using `get_var()`.

The `save_score()` function does the opposite. Note that you don't have to check if the file exists – if you try to write to a file that doesn't exist, it will be created.

Save this script and add it as an autoload in **Project Settings**:

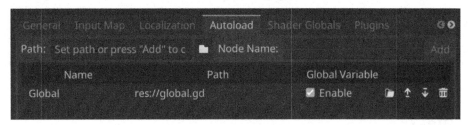

Figure 6.17: Adding a global script

Go to your `Title` scene and add another `Label` node to display the high score. Set its font and arrange it on the screen – the bottom middle might be a good choice. Add this to the script, so that the score will be displayed whenever the title screen loads:

```
func _ready():
    $Label2.text = "High Score: " + str(Global.high_score)
```

Finally, at the end of the game, you'll need to check if there's a new high score. The `score` variable is kept on the plane, so open `plane.gd` and find the `die()` function, which is called when the game ends. Add a score check and call `save_score()` if needed:

```
if score > Global.high_score:
    Global.high_score = score
    Global.save_score()
```

Run the game to test that the high score is being displayed, saved, and loaded again when you run the game the next time.

This technique can be used for any type of data that you want to save between runs of your game. It's a useful technique, so be sure to try it out with your own projects in the future. Reusing code is a great way to accelerate development, so once you've got a save system that you're happy with, stick with it!

Suggestions for additional features

For an additional challenge, try to expand the game by adding more features. Here are some suggestions to get you started:

- Track the distance the player flies in each game, and save the maximum value as a high score.
- Increase the speed incrementally as time goes on or include boost items that increase the plane's speed.
- Flying obstacles that need to be dodged, such as other planes or birds.
- (Advanced) Instead of only straight lines, add curved chunks as well. The player will have to steer and the camera will have to move to stay behind them.

This would also be a great game for you to experiment with building a game for a mobile platform. See the next chapter for information about exporting games.

Summary

In this chapter, you extended your 3D skills by learning about more of Godot's 3D nodes, such as the `CharacterBody3D`. You should have a good understanding of the 3D transform and how it works to move and rotate an object in space. Randomly generating chunks, while relatively simple in this game, is something that you can extend to much larger games and more complex environments.

Congratulations, you've made it to the end of the last project! But with these five games, your journey to becoming a game developer has just begun.

In the next chapter, you can read about some other topics that didn't quite fit into the example games, as well as find some pointers for where to go next in building your game development skills.

7

Next Steps and Additional Resources

Congratulations! The projects you've built in this book have started you on the road to becoming a Godot expert. However, you've only just scratched the surface of what's possible in Godot. As you become more proficient and the sizes of your projects grow, you'll need to know how to find solutions to your problems, how to distribute your games so they can be played, and even how to extend the engine yourself.

In this chapter, you'll learn about the following topics:

- How to effectively use Godot's built-in documentation

- Using **Git** to back up and manage your project files

- An overview of some of the vector math concepts you'll encounter in most game projects

- Using **Blender**, an open source 3D modeling application, to make 3D objects you can use in Godot

- Exporting projects to run on other platforms

- An introduction to shaders

- Using other programming languages in Godot

- Community resources where you can get help

- Becoming a Godot contributor

This chapter will help you move on from the book's projects and begin making your own games. You can use the information here to find additional resources and guidance, as well as some more advanced topics that didn't fit in with the beginner projects covered earlier.

Using Godot's documentation

Learning Godot's API can seem overwhelming at first. How can you learn about all the different nodes and the properties and methods each one contains? Fortunately, Godot's built-in documentation is there to help you. Develop the habit of using it often: it will help you find things when you're learning, but it's also a great way to quickly look up a method or property for reference once you know your way around.

> **Leveling up your skills**
>
> Learning to effectively use API documentation is the number one thing you can do to dramatically boost your skill level. Keep a docs tab open in your web browser while you're working and reference it often, looking up the nodes and/or functions you're using.

When you are in the **Script** tab of the editor, you'll see the following buttons in the upper-right corner:

Figure 7.1: Documentation buttons

The **Online Docs** button will open the documentation website in your browser. If you have a multimonitor setup, it can be very useful to keep the API reference open on one side for quick reference while you're working in Godot. For example, if you're working with a node's `position`, you can take a look at the `Vector2` document and see all of the functions available for that data type.

The other button allows you to view the documentation directly in the Godot editor. Clicking **Search Help** lets you search for any method or property name. The search is *smart*, meaning you can type part of a word and the results will be narrowed down as you type. Take a look at the following screenshot:

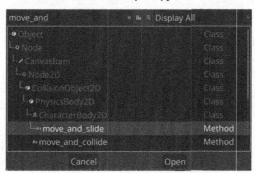

Figure 7.2: Searching for help

When you find the property or method you're looking for, click **Open** and the documentation reference for that node will appear.

Reading the API documentation

When you've found the documentation for the node you want, you'll see that it follows a common format, with the name of the node at the top followed by several subsections of information, as shown in the following screenshot:

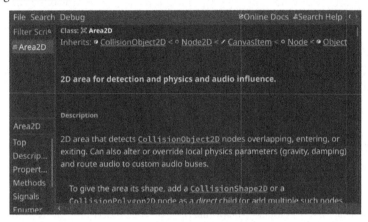

Figure 7.3: API documentation

At the top of the page is a list called **Inherits**, which shows the chain of classes that a particular node is built from, all the way back to Object, which is Godot's base object class. For example, Area2D has the following inheritance chain:

```
CollisionObject2D < Node2D < CanvasItem < Node < Object
```

This lets you quickly see what other properties this type of object may have. For example, an Area2D node has a position property because that property is defined by Node2D – any node that inherits from Node2D will also have a position in 2D space. You can click on any of the node names to jump to that node's documentation.

You can also see a list of what node types, if any, inherit from that particular node, as well as a general description of the node. Below that, you can see the member variables and methods of the node. The names of most methods and types are links, so you can click on any item to read more about it. Note that these names and descriptions are the same ones that show when you hover over a property in the Inspector.

Develop the habit of consulting the API documentation regularly as you're working. You'll find that you will quickly begin to develop a stronger understanding of how everything works together.

Version control – using Git with Godot

It happens to everyone – at a certain point, you'll make a mistake. You'll accidentally delete a file or just change some code in a way that breaks everything, but you can't figure out how to get back to the working version.

The solution to this problem is **version control software** (**VCS**). The most popular VCS, used by developers all over the world, is Git. When you use Git with your projects, every change you make is tracked, allowing you to "rewind" time at any point and recover from unwanted changes.

Fortunately, Godot is very VCS-friendly. All the content of your game is kept in the project folder. Scenes, scripts, and resources are all saved in a human-readable text format that is easy for Git to track.

Git is typically used via a command-line interface, but there are graphical clients you can use as well. There is also a Git plugin available in Godot's **AssetLib** that you can try.

In any case, the basic workflow can be broken down into two steps:

1. **Add** the files you want to track.
2. **Commit** the changes you have made.

In addition, you can use a website such as GitHub or GitLab to store and share your Git-based projects. This is a common way that developers collaborate on projects – indeed, the entire Godot source code is stored and managed on GitHub. If you're doing this, you'll have a third step: **pushing** your committed changes to the remote repository.

Most developers use the command-line version of Git, which you can install from your OS package manager or download directly from `https://git-scm.com/downloads`. There are also many GUI interfaces, such as Git Kraken or GitHub Desktop.

The details of using Git are beyond the scope of this book, but here is an example of the most basic usage: creating and updating a repository to save your changes. All of these steps will be done using your computer's terminal or command-line interface:

1. Create a new Git repository in your project folder. Navigate to the folder and type the following:

    ```
    ~/project_folder/$ git init
    ```

2. After working on your project, add the new and/or updated files to the repository by typing the following:

    ```
    ~/project_folder/$ git add *
    ```

3. Commit your changes, creating a "checkpoint" in time that you can rewind to if necessary:

    ```
    ~/project_folder/$ git commit -m "short description"
    ```

Repeat steps 2 and 3 every time you add a new feature or make changes to your project.

Make sure to type something descriptive in the commit message. If you need to rewind to a certain point in your project's history, it will help you identify the change you are looking for.

There's a lot more to Git than just the above. You can create branches – multiple versions of your game's code, collaborate with others making changes at the same time, and much more. Here are some suggestions of where you can learn more about how to use Git with your projects:

- `https://docs.github.com/en/get-started/quickstart/git-and-github-learning-resources`
- *Mastering Git* (book) by Jakub Narębski

It may seem hard at first – Git has a difficult learning curve – but it is a skill that will serve you well, and you'll really appreciate it the first time it saves you from a disaster! You may even find that Git is helpful with your non-game projects as well.

In the next section, you'll see how to use the popular Blender modeling tool to create 3D objects and use them in Godot.

Using Blender with Godot

Blender is a very popular open source 3D modeling and animation program (it does a lot of other things too). If you're planning on making a 3D game and you need to make items, characters, and environments for your game, Blender is probably your best option for doing so.

The most common workflow is to export glTF files from Blender and import them into Godot. This is a stable and reliable workflow and will work well in most situations.

When you export a glTF file, you have two options: glTF binary (`.glb`) and glTF text (`.gltf`). The binary version is more compact and is therefore the preferred format, but either will work fine.

Import hints

It's common to import meshes from Blender and then make modifications such as adding collisions or removing unneeded nodes. To simplify this, you can add suffixes to the names of your objects to give Godot a hint about how you want them to be processed on import. Here are some examples:

- `-noimp` – These objects will be removed from the imported scene.
- `-col`, `-convcol`, `-colonly` – These options tell Godot to make a collision shape from the named mesh. The first two options make a child triangle mesh or convex polygon shape, respectively. The `-colonly` option will remove the mesh entirely and replace it with a `StaticBody3D` collision.

- `-rigid` – This object will be imported as a `RigidBody3D`.

- `-loop` – Blender animations with this suffix will be imported with the loop option enabled.

See the documentation for more details on all the possible import suffixes.

Using blend files

With Godot 4, you have an additional option: importing `.blend` files directly into your Godot project. In order to use this feature, you need to have Blender installed on the same computer you're using for Godot.

To set it up, open **Editor Settings** and look under **FileSystem | Import**. Here, you can set the path where you've installed Blender.

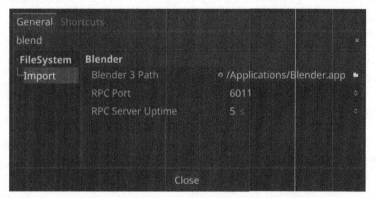

Figure 7.4: Setting up Blender support

Click the folder icon to browse to your Blender location. Once you've set this value, you can drop your `.blend` files directly into your Godot project folder. This can make prototyping and iterating your designs much faster. You can open Blender, save a change to the design, and then when you tab back to Godot, you'll instantly see it updated.

Blender is an important tool to learn if you plan on making 3D games. Because of its open source nature, it's a great fit for working with Godot. While its learning curve can be challenging, investing time in learning it will give you a huge benefit when designing and building 3D games.

Now that you've explored how to import external content into your game project, the next section will explain how you can export your game to run on other systems, such as mobile devices, PCs, or the web.

Exporting projects

Eventually, your project will reach the stage where you want to share it with the world. Exporting your project means converting it into a package that can be run by someone who doesn't have the Godot editor. You can export your project to a number of popular platforms.

Godot supports the following target platforms:

- Android (mobile)

- iOS (mobile)

- Linux

- macOS

- HTML5 (web)

- Windows Desktop

- UWP (Windows Universal)

The requirements for exporting a project vary depending on the platform you are targeting. For example, to export to iOS, you must be running on a macOS computer with Xcode installed.

Each platform is unique, and some features of your game may not work on some platforms because of hardware limitations, screen size, or other factors. As an example, if you wanted to export the *Coin Dash* game for an Android phone, your player wouldn't be able to move because the user wouldn't have a keyboard! For that platform, you would need to include touchscreen controls in your game's code (more about this later).

Every platform is unique, and there are many factors to consider when configuring your project for export. Consult the official documentation for the latest instructions on exporting to your desired platform.

Exporting for consoles

While it's perfectly possible for Godot games to run on consoles such as Switch or Xbox, the process is more complex. Console companies such as Nintendo and Microsoft require the developer to sign a contract that includes a secrecy clause. That means that, while you can make your game run on the console, you can't share the code you wrote to make it work publicly. If you do plan to release your game on a console platform, you'll either need to do that work yourself or partner with a company that has already entered such an agreement.

Getting the export templates

Export templates are versions of Godot that are compiled for each target platform but don't include the editor. Your project will be combined with the target platform's template to create a standalone application.

To begin, you must download the export templates. Select **Manage Export Templates** from the **Editor** menu:

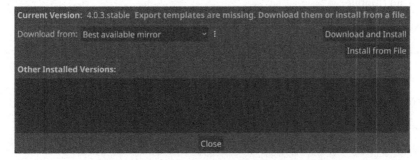

Figure 7.5: Manage Export Templates

In this window, you can click **Download and Install** to fetch the export templates matching the version of Godot you are using. If you're running multiple versions of Godot for some reason, you'll see the other versions listed in the window.

Export presets

When you're ready to export your project, click on **Project | Export**.

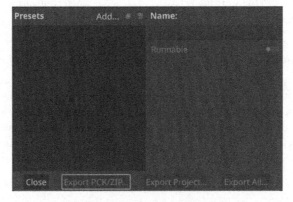

Figure 7.6: Export settings

In this window, you can create **presets** for each platform by clicking **Add...** and selecting the platform from the list. You can make as many presets for each platform as you wish. For example, you may want to create both "debug" and "release" versions of your projects.

Each platform has its own settings and options – too many to describe here. The default values are typically good, but you should test them thoroughly before distributing the project. Consult the official documentation at `https://docs.godotengine.org/` for details.

Exporting

There are two export buttons at the bottom of the export window. The first button, **Export PCK/ZIP...**, will only create a PCK, or packed, version of your project's data. This doesn't include an executable, so the game can't be run on its own. This method is useful if you need to provide add-ons, updates, or **downloadable content (DLC)** for your game.

The second button, **Export Project...**, will create an executable version of your game, such as an .exe for Windows or an .apk for Android.

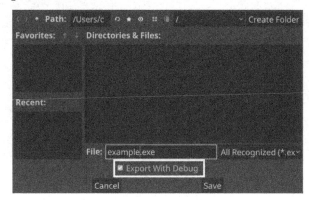

Figure 7.7: Export dialog

In the next dialog, you can choose where to save your exported project. Take note of the **Export with Debug** checkbox, which is checked by default. You'll want to disable this when it is time to export the final, released version of your game.

Exporting for specific platforms

The exact steps and requirements for exporting vary depending on your target platform. For example, exporting to desktop platforms (Windows, MacOS, Linux) is very straightforward and will work without any additional configuration.

Exporting on mobile platforms, however, can be more complex. To export for Android, for example, you'll need to install Google's Android Studio and configure it correctly. The detailed requirements can change regularly as mobile platforms update, so you should check the Godot documentation at this link for the most accurate information: `https://docs.godotengine.org/en/latest/tutorials/export/`

Once you've configured the platforms you wish to export, the window will look like this:

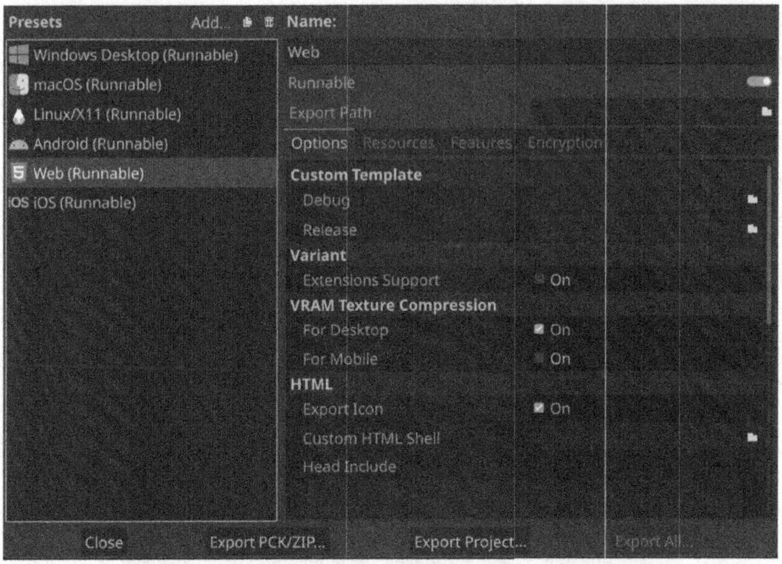

Figure 7.8: Ready to export

Godot's export system is comprehensive and robust. You can manage multiple versions, export different features for different platforms, and many other options. While it may seem complex at first, remember that the complexity mostly comes from the rules of a particular platform. It's best if you practice with desktop platforms first before attempting to work with mobile.

In the next section, you'll learn about how visual effects are implemented using a special type of program called a shader.

Introduction to shaders

A **shader** is a program that is designed to run on the GPU and alters the way that objects appear on the screen. Shaders are used extensively in both 2D and 3D development to create a variety of visual effects. They are called shaders because they were originally used for shading and lighting effects, but today they are used for a wide variety of visual effects. Because they run in the GPU in *parallel*, they are very fast but also come with some restrictions.

> **Learning more**
>
> This section is a very brief introduction to the concept of shaders. For a more in-depth understanding, see https://thebookofshaders.com/ and Godot's shader documentation at https://docs.godotengine.org/en/latest/tutorials/shaders/.

Earlier in this book, when you added a `StandardMaterial3D` to a mesh, you were actually adding a shader – one that's pre-configured and built into Godot. It's great for many common situations, but sometimes you need something more specific, and for that, you'll need to write shader code.

In Godot, you'll write shaders in a language very similar to GLSL ES 3.0. If you are familiar with C-style languages, you'll find the syntax very similar. If you are not, it may look strange to you at first. See the end of this section for links to further resources where you can learn more.

Shaders in Godot come in several types:

- **spatial** (for 3D rendering)
- **canvas_item** (for 2D rendering)
- **particles** (for rendering particle effects)
- **sky** (for rendering 3D sky materials)
- **fog** (for rendering volumetric fog effects)

The first line of your shader must declare which of these types you are writing. Typically, this will be automatically filled in for you when you add a shader to a particular type of node.

After determining the type of shader, you can then choose what phase(s) of the rendering process you want to affect:

- **Fragment** shaders are used to set the color of all affected pixels
- **Vertex** shaders can modify the vertices of a shape or mesh, changing its apparent shape
- **Light** shaders are applied to alter the way light is processed for an object

For each of these three shader types, you will write code that will be run *simultaneously* on every affected item. This is where the real power of shaders comes from. For example, when using a fragment shader, the code is run on every pixel of the object at the same time. This is a very different process than what you might be used to using a traditional language, where you would loop over each pixel one at a time. That kind of sequential code just isn't fast enough to handle the huge number of pixels modern games need to process.

The importance of the GPU

Consider a game running at the relatively low resolution of 480 x 720 – a typical phone resolution. The total number of pixels on the screen is almost 350,000. Any manipulation of those pixels in code must happen in less than 1/60 of a second to avoid lag – even less when you consider the rest of your code that also has to run on every frame: game logic, animation, networking, and everything else. This is why GPUs are so important, especially for high-end games that may be processing millions of pixels each and every frame.

Creating a 2D shader

To demonstrate some shader effects, create a scene with a `Sprite2D` node and choose any texture you like. This demo will use the player image from *Coin Dash*:

Figure 7.9: Player sprite

A shader can be added to any `CanvasItem` derived node – in this case, `Sprite2D`, via its **Material** property. In this property, select **New ShaderMaterial** and click on the newly created resource.

Figure 7.10: Adding a shader material

The first property is **Shader**, where you can choose **New Shader**. When you do, a **Create Shader** panel appears.

Figure 7.11: Create Shader options

Note that **Mode** is already showing the correct shader type, but you'll need to supply a filename for the shader. By default, Godot shader files end in .gdshader. Click **Create** and then you can click your new shader to edit it in the bottom panel.

Your new shader has the following code by default:

```
shader_type canvas_item;

void fragment() {
    // Place fragment code here.
}
```

Shader functions have a number of **built-ins**, which are either input values or output values. For example, the TEXTURE input built-in contains the pixel data of the object's texture, while the COLOR output built-in is used to set the pixel color. Remember, the code in the fragment shader will affect the color of every processed pixel.

When working with shaders in the TEXTURE property, for example, coordinates are measured in a *normalized* (that is, ranging from 0 to 1) coordinate space. This coordinate space is called UV to distinguish it from the x/y coordinate space.

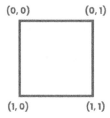

Figure 7.12: UV coordinate space

As a very small example, our first shader will change the color of each pixel in the image based on its UV position.

Type the following code into the **Shader Editor** panel:

```
shader_type canvas_item;

void fragment() {
COLOR = vec4(UV.x, UV.y, 0.0, 1.0);
}
```

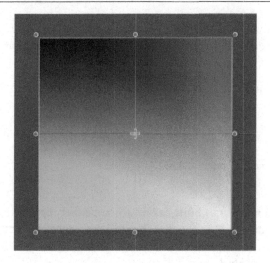

Figure 7.13: Color gradient

As soon as you do this, you'll see the entire image change to a gradient of red and green. What happened? Look at the preceding UV image – as we move from left to right, the red value increases from 0 to 1, and the green does the same from bottom to top.

Let's try another example. This time, to allow you to choose the color, you can use a uniform variable.

Uniforms allow you to pass data into the shader from outside. Declaring a uniform variable will cause it to appear in the Inspector (similar to the way @export works in GDScript) and also allows you to set it via code:

```
shader_type canvas_item;

uniform vec4 fill_color : source_color;

void fragment() {
    COLOR = fill_color;
}
```

You'll see that **Fill Color** has appeared under **Shader Parameters** in the Inspector, and you can change its value.

Figure 7.14: Shader Parameters

Why did the entire rectangle of the image change color in these examples? Because the output COLOR is applied to every pixel. Our player image has transparent pixels surrounding it, so we can ignore those by not changing the pixel's a value:

```
COLOR.rgb = fill_color.rgb;
```

Now we can change the color of the object. Let's turn it into a "hit" effect so that we can make the object flash whenever it's hit:

```
shader_type canvas_item;

uniform vec4 fill_color : source_color;
uniform bool active = false;

void fragment() {
    if (active == true) {
        COLOR.rgb = fill_color.rgb;
    }
}
```

Note that now you can toggle the color on and off by clicking the **Active** property. Since both uniform variables appear in the **Inspector**, you could now add a track to an AnimationPlayer that animates these values for your visual effect.

Here's another example. This time, we'll create an outline around the image:

```
shader_type canvas_item;

uniform vec4 line_color : source_color;
uniform float line_thickness : hint_range(0, 10) = 0.5;
```

```
void fragment() {
    vec2 size = TEXTURE_PIXEL_SIZE * line_thickness;
    float outline = texture(TEXTURE, UV + vec2(-size.x,
        0)).a;
    outline += texture(TEXTURE, UV + vec2(0, size.y)).a;
    outline += texture(TEXTURE, UV + vec2(size.x, 0)).a;
    outline += texture(TEXTURE, UV + vec2(0, -size.y)).a;
    outline = min(outline, 1.0);

    vec4 color = texture(TEXTURE, UV);
    COLOR = mix(color, line_color, outline - color.a);
}
```

In this shader, we have a lot more going on. We're using the built-in TEXTURE_PIXEL_SIZE to get the normalized size of each pixel (its size compared to the size of the image). Then, we get a float value that "adds up" how transparent the pixels on all four sides of the image are. Finally, we use the mix() function to combine the original pixel's color with the line color based on that outline value.

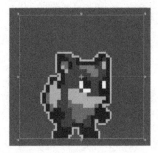

Figure 7.15: Outline shader

An important thing to note – did you notice that the outline did not go below the character's feet? This is because an object's shader can only affect the pixels of that image. Since the character's feet in this image are on the edge, there are no pixels available below them that can be affected by the shader. It's important to keep this in mind when working on 2D shader effects. If you're creating 2D art, leave a border of a few pixels around the image to prevent clipping at the edges.

3D shaders

Let's try one 3D shader so you can see how the vertex() shader works. In a new scene, add a MeshInstance3D with a PlaneMesh shape. So that you can see the vertices better, select **Display Wireframe** from the **Perspective** menu.

Click the **Mesh** resource to expand it and add a new shader in the **Material** property, just like you did previously.

Figure 7.16: Adding a shader to the plane

Since we're using a plane shape, we have four vertices: the four corners of the shape. The vertex() function will apply an effect to each of these vertices. For example, adding to their y value would move them all upward.

Let's start with this code:

```
shader_type spatial;

void vertex() {
    VERTEX.y += sin(10.0 * UV.x) * 0.5;
}
```

Note that we're using a spatial type shader now, since our node is a Node3D.

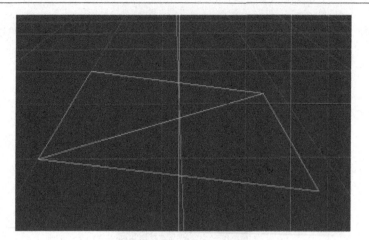

Figure 7.17: Shifting the vertices

It doesn't look like much changed – the two vertices in the +X direction moved down a little bit. But UV.x is only either 0 or 1, so the sin() function doesn't have much to do. To see more variation, we need to add more vertices. In the mesh properties, change both **Subdivide Width** and **Subdivide Depth** to 32.

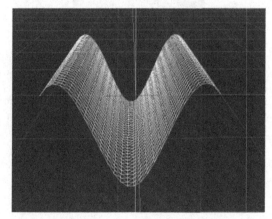

Figure 7.18: Working with more vertices

Now we can see much more variation in the effect, as the different vertices along the *x* axis are moved up or down in a smooth sine wave.

For one more fun effect, let's use the TIME built-in to animate the effect. Change the code to this:

```
VERTEX.y += sin(TIME + 10.0 * UV.x) * 0.5;
```

Take some time to experiment with this. Don't be afraid to try things – experimentation is a great way to become more comfortable with how shaders work.

Learning more

Shaders are capable of an amazing range of effects. Experimenting with Godot's shader language is a great way to learn the basics. The best place to start is with the shader section of Godot's documentation:

`https://docs.godotengine.org/en/latest/tutorials/shaders/`

There is also a wealth of resources on the internet for learning more. When learning about shaders, you can use resources that aren't specific to Godot, and you shouldn't have much trouble getting them to work in Godot. The concept is the same across all types of graphics applications.

In addition, Godot's documentation includes a page on converting shaders from other popular sources into Godot's version of GLSL.

To see some examples of just how powerful shaders can be, visit `https://www.shadertoy.com/`.

This section was only a brief introduction to the in-depth topic of shaders and shader effects. While it can be a very challenging subject to master, the power it gives you makes it well worth the effort.

In the next section, you'll see how it's possible to use other programming languages with Godot.

Using other programming languages in Godot

The projects in this book have all been written using GDScript. GDScript has a number of advantages that make it the best choice for building your games. It is very tightly integrated with Godot's API, and its Python-style syntax makes it useful for rapid development while also being very beginner-friendly.

It's not the only option, however. Godot also supports two other "official" scripting languages and also provides tools for integrating code using a variety of other languages.

C#

C# is very popular in game development, and the Godot version is based on the .NET 6.0 framework. Because of its wide use, there are many resources available for learning C# and a great deal of existing code in the language for accomplishing a variety of game-related functions.

At the time of writing, Godot version 4.0 is still relatively new. Features are being added and bugs are being fixed continuously, so see the C# documentation at this link to get the latest information: `https://docs.godotengine.org/en/stable/tutorials/scripting/c_sharp/index.html`

If you want to try out the C# implementation, you'll need to first make sure you have the .NET SDK installed, which you can get from `https://dotnet.microsoft.com/download`. You must also download the Godot version that has C# support included, which you can find at `http://godotengine.org/download`, where it is labeled **Godot Engine - .NET**.

You'll also need to use an external editor – such as Visual Studio Code or MonoDevelop – that provides more debugging and language functionality than Godot's built-in editor. You can set this in **Editor Settings** under the **Dotnet** section.

To attach a C# script to a node, select the language from the **Attach Node Script** dialog:

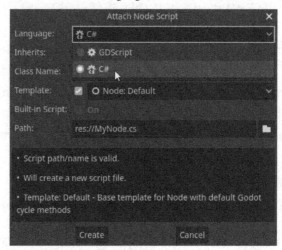

Figure 7.19: Create script dialog

In general, scripting in C# works very much the same as what you've already done in GDScript. The main difference is that the API functions are renamed in PascalCase to follow C# standards instead of the snake_case that's standard for GDScript.

There are also a number of existing C# libraries that you may find useful in building your game. Things such as procedural generation, artificial intelligence, or other intensive topics may be easier to implement using available C# libraries.

Here's an example of CharacterBody2D movement in C#. Compare this with the movement script in *Jungle Jump*:

```csharp
using Godot;

public partial class MyCharacterBody2D : CharacterBody2D
{
    private float _speed = 100.0f;
    private float _jumpSpeed = -400.0f;

    // Get the gravity from the project settings so you can
        sync with rigid body nodes.
    public float Gravity = ProjectSettings.GetSetting(
        "physics/2d/default_gravity").AsSingle();
```

```
    public override void _PhysicsProcess(double delta)
    {
        Vector2 velocity = Velocity;

        // Add the gravity.
        velocity.Y += Gravity * (float)delta;

        // Handle jump.
        if (Input.IsActionJustPressed("jump") &&
        IsOnFloor())
            velocity.Y = _jumpSpeed;

        // Get the input direction.
        Vector2 direction = Input.GetAxis("ui_left",
            "ui_right");
        velocity.X = direction * _speed;

        Velocity = velocity;
        MoveAndSlide();
    }
}
```

For more details about setting up and using C#, see the **Scripting** section of the documentation linked above.

Other languages – GDExtension

There are many programming languages to choose from. Each has its strengths and weaknesses, as well as its fans who prefer to use it over other options. While it doesn't make sense to support every language directly in Godot, there are situations where GDScript is not sufficient to solve a particular problem. Perhaps you want to use an existing external library, or you're doing something computationally intensive – such as AI or procedural world generation – that it doesn't make sense to write in GDScript.

Because GDScript is an interpreted language, it trades performance for flexibility. This means that for some processor-intensive code, it can run unacceptably slow. In this case, the highest performance would be achieved by running native code written in a compiled language. In this situation, you can move that code to GDExtension.

GDExtension is a technology that opens up the same API available to GDScript and C#, making it possible to write code in other languages that talks to Godot. By default, it works directly with C and C++, but by using **third-party bindings**, you can use it with many other languages.

At the time of writing, several projects are available that use GDExtension to allow you to use other languages for scripting. These include C, C++, Rust, Python, Nim, and others. While these additional language bindings are still relatively new at the time of writing, they each have a dedicated group of developers working on them. If you're interested in using a particular language with Godot, a Google search of "godot + <language name>" will help you find what's available.

Working with other programming languages is certainly not required for just about any game project you may encounter, so don't feel that it's something you need to learn if it's foreign to you. It's presented here for those to whom it might be useful, and it's something to keep in mind if you have a preferred language you'd like to work with.

In the next section, you can explore the community resources that are available for you to learn more about how Godot works, find examples, and even get help with your own projects.

Getting help – community resources

Godot's online community is one of its strengths. Because of its open source nature, there is a wide variety of people working together to improve the engine, write documentation, and help each other with issues.

You can find a list of official community resources at `https://godotengine.org/community`. These links may change over time, but the following are the main community resources you should be aware of:

- **GitHub** – `https://github.com/godotengine/`

  The Godot GitHub repository is where Godot's developers work. You can find Godot's source code there if you find yourself needing to compile a custom version of the engine for your own use or if you're just curious how things work under the hood.

  If you find any kind of problem with the engine itself – something that doesn't work, a typo in the documentation, and so on – this is the place where you should report it.

- **Godot Q&A** – `https://godotengine.org/qa/`

  This is Godot's official help site. You can post questions here for the community to answer, as well as searching the growing database of previously answered questions. If you happen to see a question you know the answer to, you can help out as well.

- **Discord** – `https://discord.gg/zH7NUgz`

  The Godot Engine Discord is a very active and welcoming community of Godot users where you can get help, find answers to questions, and discuss your project with others. You may even encounter the author of this book hanging out in the #beginner channel, answering questions!

Godot Recipes

I have also created the **Godot Recipes** website at `https://godotrecipes.com/`. This is a collection of solutions and examples to help you make any game system you might need. You can see how to make an FPS character, handle complex animation states, or add AI to your enemies.

There are also additional tutorials and examples of completed games that you can try out.

Figure 7.20: Godot Recipes website

As illustrated by this section, one of the great strengths of the Godot Engine is its community. The resources listed here, along with many others, are built by the community of Godot users who are passionate about the engine and about helping others. In the next section, you can find out how you can contribute to Godot as well.

Contributing to Godot

Godot is an open source, community-driven project. All of the work that's done to build, test, document, and otherwise support Godot is done primarily by passionate individuals contributing their time and skills. For the majority of contributors, it is a labor of love, and they take pride in helping to build something of quality that people enjoy using.

In order for Godot to continue growing and improving, there is always a need for more members of the community to step up and contribute. There are many ways you can help out, regardless of your skill level or the amount of time you can commit.

Contributing to the engine

There are two main ways you can directly contribute to Godot's development. If you visit `https://github.com/godotengine/godot`, you can see Godot's source code, as well as finding out exactly what's being worked on. Click the **Clone** or **Download** button, and you'll have the up-to-the-minute source code and can test out the latest features. You'll need to build the engine, but don't be intimidated: Godot is one of the easiest open source projects to compile that you'll find. See `https://docs.godotengine.org/en/latest/contributing/development/compiling/index.html` for instructions.

If you're not able to actually contribute to the C++ code, go to the **Issues** tab, where you can report or read about bugs and suggestions for improvements. There is always a need for people to confirm bug reports, test fixes, and give their opinions on new features.

Writing documentation

Godot's official documentation is only as good as its community's contributions. From something as small as correcting a typo to writing an entire tutorial, all levels of help are very welcome. The home of the official documentation is `https://github.com/godotengine/godot-docs`.

Hopefully, by now, you've taken some time to browse through the official documentation and get an idea of what's available. If you spot something wrong or something missing, open an issue at the aforementioned GitHub link. If you're comfortable with using GitHub, you can even go ahead and submit a pull request yourself. Just make sure you read all the guidelines first so that your contribution will be accepted. You can find the guidelines at `https://docs.godotengine.org/en/latest/contributing/ways_to_contribute.html`.

If you speak a language other than English, translations are also very much needed and will be greatly appreciated by Godot's non-English-speaking users. See `https://docs.godotengine.org/en/latest/contributing/documentation/editor_and_docs_localization` for how to contribute in your language.

Donations

Godot is a not-for-profit project, and user donations go a long way to help pay for hosting costs and development resources, such as hardware. Financial contributions also allow the project to pay core developers, allowing them to dedicate themselves part- or full-time to working on the engine.

The easiest way to contribute to Godot is via the donation page at `https://godotengine.org/donate`.

Summary

In this chapter, you learned about a few additional topics that will help you continue to level up your Godot skills. Godot has a great many features in addition to those explored in this book. You'll need to know where to look and where to ask for help as you move on to working on projects of your own.

You also learned about some more advanced topics, such as working with other programming languages and using shaders to enhance your game's visual effects.

In addition, since Godot is built by its community, you learned how you could participate and become part of the team that is making it one of the fastest-growing projects of its kind.

Final words

Thank you for taking the time to read this book. I hope you found it useful in starting your game development journey with Godot. The goal of this book was not to give you a "copy-and-paste" solution to making games but rather to help you develop an intuition for the process of game development. As you'll see when you explore other resources, there are often many ways to solve a problem, and there may not be a single "right" answer. It's up to you as a developer to evaluate and determine what works for you in your situation. I wish you luck in your future game projects, and I hope to play them sometime in the future!

Index

Symbols

W

Y

Z

www.packtpub.com

Subscribe to our online digital library for full access to over 7,000 books and videos, as well as industry leading tools to help you plan your personal development and advance your career. For more information, please visit our website.

Why subscribe?

- Spend less time learning and more time coding with practical eBooks and Videos from over 4,000 industry professionals

- Improve your learning with Skill Plans built especially for you

- Get a free eBook or video every month

- Fully searchable for easy access to vital information

- Copy and paste, print, and bookmark content

Did you know that Packt offers eBook versions of every book published, with PDF and ePub files available? You can upgrade to the eBook version at packtpub.com and as a print book customer, you are entitled to a discount on the eBook copy. Get in touch with us at customercare@packtpub.com for more details.

At www.packtpub.com, you can also read a collection of free technical articles, sign up for a range of free newsletters, and receive exclusive discounts and offers on Packt books and eBooks.

Other Books You May Enjoy

If you enjoyed this book, you may be interested in these other books by Packt:

Game Development with Blender and Godot

Kumsal Obuz

ISBN: 978-1-80181-602-1

- Discover what low-poly modeling is and why it matters
- Understand how to use materials, shaders, and textures in your models
- Explore how to render and animate a scene in Blender
- Focus on how to export Blender assets and import them into Godot
- Use 3D low-poly models in Godot to create fun games
- Design a dynamic and easy-to-navigate game world
- Explore how to interact with the game via interfaces
- Understand how to export your game for Windows

Godot 4 Game Development Cookbook

Jeff Johnson

ISBN: 978-1-83882-607-9

- Speed up 2D game development with new TileSet and TileMap updates
- Improve 2D and 3D rendering with the Vulkan Renderer
- Master the new animation editor in Godot 4 for advanced game development
- Enhance visuals and performance with visual shaders and the updated shader language
- Import Blender blend files into Godot to optimize your workflow
- Explore new physics system additions for improved realism and behavior of game objects
- Experience innovative features by building multiplayer games in Godot 4

Packt is searching for authors like you

If you're interested in becoming an author for Packt, please visit `authors.packtpub.com` and apply today. We have worked with thousands of developers and tech professionals, just like you, to help them share their insight with the global tech community. You can make a general application, apply for a specific hot topic that we are recruiting an author for, or submit your own idea.

Hi!

Hi, it's Chris Bradfield, author of *Godot 4 Game Development Projects*. I really hope you enjoyed reading this book and found it helpful to get started with Godot and game development.

It would really help us (and other potential readers!) if you could leave a review on Amazon sharing your thoughts on how this book helped you get started with Godot.

Go to the link below or scan the QR code to leave your review:

`https://packt.link/r/1804610402`

Your review will help us to understand what's worked well in this book, and what could be improved upon for future editions, so it really is appreciated.

Best wishes,

Chris Bradfield

Download a free PDF copy of this book

Thanks for purchasing this book!

Do you like to read on the go but are unable to carry your print books everywhere?

Is your eBook purchase not compatible with the device of your choice?

Don't worry, now with every Packt book you get a DRM-free PDF version of that book at no cost.

Read anywhere, any place, on any device. Search, copy, and paste code from your favorite technical books directly into your application.

The perks don't stop there, you can get exclusive access to discounts, newsletters, and great free content in your inbox daily

Follow these simple steps to get the benefits:

1. Scan the QR code or visit the link below

https://packt.link/free-ebook/9781804610404

1. Submit your proof of purchase
2. That's it! We'll send your free PDF and other benefits to your email directly

Made in the USA
Las Vegas, NV
07 June 2024

90832636R00149